How To Be Smart
With Your Time

How To Be Smart With Your Time

Duncan Bannatyne

© Bannatyne Media Ltd 2010

The right of Duncan Bannatyne to be identified
as the author of this work has been asserted in
accordance with the Copyright, Designs and
Patents Act 1988.

First published in Great Britain in 2010
by Orion Books
An imprint of the Orion Publishing Group Ltd
Orion House, 5 Upper St Martin's Lane,
London, WC2H 9EA
An Hachette Livre Company

3 5 7 9 10 8 6 4 2

A CIP catalogue record for this book
is available from the British Library.

ISBN 978 1 4091 1288 4

Printed and bound in the UK by CPI Mackays, Chatham ME5 8TD

The Orion publishing group's policy is to use papers
that are natural, renewable and recyclable products and
made from wood grown in sustainable forests. The logging
and manufacturing processes are expected to conform to
the environmental regulations of the country of origin.

www.orionbooks.co.uk

Contents

PART ONE — WHAT ARE YOU DOING WITH YOUR LIFE?

PART TWO — WHAT ARE YOU DOING TODAY?

TO MY CHILDREN

Abigail, Hollie, Jennifer, Eve, Emily and Tom

Remember I love you more . . .

Acknowledgements

First and foremost I would like to thank my beautiful wife, Joanne, and my children, Abigail, Hollie, Jennifer, Eve, Emily, Tom and not forgetting my grandchild Ava. Thank you and I love you all so much.

I would like to thank Jo Monroe for working with me a fourth time; it has been an absolute pleasure. Thanks also to Alan Samson at the Orion Publishing Group and Jonny Geller at Curtis Brown; your help with this book has been invaluable.

A big thank you to everyone.

Foreword

One of the reasons I make the most of every day is because I lost my sister Helen unexpectedly, and tragically, when she was just twenty-five years old. People who have been bereaved can no longer pretend that they've got all the time in the world and I am always aware that anything can happen to any of us at any time. There is almost nothing as important as making the most of whatever time we have, because none of us knows when it's going to run out. What I do know, however, is that when my time's up I don't want to be saying to myself 'I wish I'd done . . .' This might look like a book about time management, but it's really about fulfilling your dreams and living a life without regret. It shouldn't take a tragedy for us to realise just how precious time is.

Duncan Bannatyne

Introduction

Time, unlike money, opportunity or good looks, is the one resource that is allocated equally to all of us. No matter what our financial or personal situation, we each get twenty-four hours a day, which is why spending your time more efficiently can transform your life. I've heard it said that no man is rich enough to buy back his past, and that's why I think time is the single most precious resource any individual, or any company, has. Managing it purposefully doesn't just mean you can do more, it means you can *achieve* more.

So many people claim that they don't have enough hours in the day. Whether they're making excuses as to why they haven't launched the business they've been promising to start, or written the book they've been talking about for years, or just haven't put a load of washing on when they said they would, the answer is usually that they've run out of time. What they might not realise is that if you run out of time for long enough, you'll actually run out of life! That's why I think learning to manage your time is fundamental to living a life that's free of regrets.

The skills in this book will help you find the time to do the things that matter to you. However, this isn't a book about doing things slightly quicker, or multi-tasking (I'm a man, and my wife tells me it's not in my nature!) to save ten minutes here and there; that's about connecting with goals and aspirations that will drive you forward with such speed that you will naturally become more efficient.

There are plenty of time-management books on the shelf, but most of them seem to be about clearing backlogs of emails and filing paperwork. The problem with this approach is that it assumes your lack of time, and possibly your lack of success, can be solved with the office equivalent of a spring clean. Yet millions of jobs don't involve paperwork and even retired people I know tell me that they still can't find the time to spend on things that really matter to them. The solution to freeing up time isn't by tinkering with individual tasks and processes – it's by dealing with the fundamental reasons why you're not motivated to find the time to do the things that count.

Unlike the books that focus on streamlining tasks to create free time, I'm going to take a different approach. I think that it's only when you know what you're doing with your life that you can work out what you're going to do with your day. I know this because I spent most of my twenties as a beach bum in Jersey. I took odd jobs and, as long as I had enough money to buy a round of drinks, I was happy. I truly don't regret a single day I spent partying and chasing girls, but as I approached my thirtieth birthday I realised I wanted to start a family, and that meant taking life a little more seriously.

With no qualifications and no prospects, I realised that the best chance I had of making money was to work for myself. I looked around for opportunities and, while I was waiting for the right one, I stockpiled cash from a job in a bakery where I worked nights so that during the day I could do up cars I'd bought cheaply at auction. I quickly got the deposit together to buy a house. Shortly afterwards, I spotted the opportunity to start a business with an ice-cream van that came up at auction: from that moment on I was fired up to make as much money as possible as quickly as possible so that I could get home to my family.

The difference between me at twenty-eight and me at thirty was incredible, and I can see now that the reason behind that difference was simple: I had a goal. It was a pretty simple goal: all I wanted was to raise my children in a decent house and give them opportunities I'd never had as a kid, yet this drove me to make the most of every day. I had gone from being the kind of guy who would put off whatever he could until tomorrow to being the kind of man who got stuff done. That's why the first part of this book is about identifying your goals and the second half is about using them to motivate you to tackle and complete the kinds of tasks you would otherwise avoid or put off, thereby freeing up time to pursue the things that matter.

Since I started my first business, I have found that a lot of the processes I apply to my companies can also be applied to my home life to make me more efficient. Over the years, I have learnt that the mechanisms businesses use to measure profitability – things like SWOT analyses (see Chapter 13, p. 69), cost:benefit assessments, risk evaluation and other bits of jargon I'll explain as I go along – can be used by individuals to make themselves more time-efficient.

I hate wasting time more than I hate wasting money. There's not much I resent more than being made to sit through dull meetings or getting stuck in traffic and I would rather take the stairs than wait for a lift. Being in business for the past thirty years has taught me a great deal about efficiency, and by applying standard business practices to your use of time, you too can be smarter with your time. I see time as a form of currency that can be invested wisely or squandered foolishly. You can fritter it away on pointless activities with very low rates of return, or you can spend it sensibly on activities that bring satisfaction and benefits. Learning the secrets of time management will allow you to do just that.

The work/life balance

There have been times in my life when I have worked eighteen hours a day, seven days a week for months at a stretch. There have also been times in my life when spending five hours in the office each week has been enough to oversee my businesses because I have delegated the day-to-day running to my managing director. At different stages of your life, it makes sense to do different things with your time. At thirty-five, if I had had an extra hour in the day I would have spent it growing my business. These days I would spend it with my wife and kids.

I am not about to advocate that a busy life is better than a leisurely one, or vice versa, or suggest that you try and replicate the patterns of my life; the key thing I want to get across is that *you* have to be sure that whatever *you* do today is in line with *your* longer-term ambitions. It doesn't matter if you're busy – in fact busyness can be very ineffective – or not; what matters is that you get the things done that you need to get done. At different stages in your life you will have different priorities and there is no right and no wrong way to spend your time. If your ambition is to play PlayStation games, then any time you spend on your PlayStation is time well spent. If, however, you aspire to something else, time spent on PlayStation is pretty much wasted.

I've placed statistics throughout the book about how we use our time, and when you see how much time we fritter away I hope you'll be encouraged to start using your time more purposefully. Some of the statistics have been carried out by marketing agencies hoping to promote a particular product so they may not be entirely scientific, but the findings from different surveys keep coming up with the same data, the same findings – we are simply throwing our lives away on things that don't matter.

There are 168 hours in a week. Let's say you sleep eight hours a night and work a forty-hour week: that leaves you with seventy-two hours a week to potentially call your own. That's a whole three days, which means over 40% of your week is yours to make a difference with. However, whether it's our partners, our bosses, our colleagues, our kids or our bank managers making demands on us, it can often feel as if our time isn't our own. The tools in this book will help you reclaim as much of that time as possible.

I've come to see that the secret to a happy and fulfilled life lies in the answers to two fundamental questions –

1   **What are you doing with your life?**

2   **What are you doing today?**

– and this book is all about helping you come up with the answers. I've divided the book into two sections to deal with those two questions. The first helps you paint the bigger picture and the second sets out how small changes in your daily life can help you achieve more in the long term. Without a good answer to the first question, it's hard to know how you should be answering the second question. Some of the exercises in this book will require you to do some serious soul-searching to come up with honest answers, but the short amount of time spent on them will pay enormous dividends in the near future. It might help if you see this book as the equivalent of a diet book: instead of scrutinising your relationship with food, you are going to reassess your relationship with time.

Being smart with your time is about balancing your long-term goals with your short-term needs. By mastering a few basic concepts you will be able to get what you want out of life and have enough time left over to get more of it. Throughout this book, whether I'm talking long term or short term, there are three fundamental concepts you need to get to grips with:

1 Compromise

This will come up time and again. You won't always be able to do everything and some of the things you can do won't always be done to the standards you had hoped. Much of making the most of your time is underwritten by knowing when to compromise. Perfectionism takes too much time.

2 Focus

When you have identified your goals, it is vital that you find a way to focus on making sure they are achieved. Whether it's switching off your phone to get a report written or turning down invitations to spend time on your chosen goals, learning to focus can transform how much you can achieve.

3 Decision-making

Throughout this book I will be asking you to make decisions – some may be quite trivial while others will be fundamental – and the quicker you make them, the faster you can move on. Being indecisive squanders time and opportunity and is the enemy of progress. The good news is, the more decisions you make and stick to, the better you become at making better choices.

These might not be the skills you thought you'd get from a book on time management, but, if you master them, they will transform your life more profoundly and more rapidly than getting to grips with your paperwork. But I've got plenty of advice on that, too . . .

What are you doing with your life?

1
Identify your goals

How can you go about getting what you want if you don't know what it is? Having a goal in life is the best motivator to get you up in the morning and keep you fired up throughout the day. Without goals, we drift and become aimless. To put it simply, we waste time.

Most of us do have a goal. We often have a pretty good idea of the kind of career we'd like, or the kinds of holidays we'd like to take, or the kind of home we'd like to live in; but every day events rise up like barriers between us and our goals and we become disconnected from them. Sometimes we let ourselves drift away from our goals because our ambitions have changed without us noticing: we no longer want the same things we used to want, but, because we haven't recognised this, our goals lose their ability to drive us forward, and then we fail to replace the old goals with new ambitions that would inspire us.

So whether you fall between 'I haven't got a clue what I want do with my life' or 'I know what I was born to do', I encourage you to work through this first exercise methodically. There are going to be quite a few exercises throughout this book, and you may find it helpful to start a new notebook so that you can keep all of your notes in one place.

EXERCISE 1 – **Your ideal life**

I want you to spend the next little while imagining your ideal life. I'm going to take you through a series of prompts to get you thinking logically and laterally about the kind of life you really want, and all I want you to do is write down a few sentences for each of the categories. I'm going to assume that everyone wants to be healthy, as without our health we can't do much else. This is about using your imagination and should be quite good fun, and it doesn't matter at this stage if your ambitions for different aspects of your life are contradictory.

Your home

Where do you want to live? Some people want to live in a New York loft apartment, some people want to live round the corner from their mum, while others fancy a lodge in the woods or a villa by the sea. Think seriously about the kind of place you want to live in – how many bedrooms has it got, how big is the garden, is it in a city centre, or isolated in rolling countryside?

Now that you've let your imagination run riot, apply a little reality check and ask yourself if you'd be happy in your chosen place. Do you need it to be close to schools, or shops or family? You may be wondering why I'm not asking you whether or not you think you'll ever be able to afford it: that's because I know if living in a home like the one you're imagining is enough of a goal, you'll find a way of affording it. All that matters at this stage is that not only have you dreamt up your ideal pad, but you also know that you would be truly happy living in it. Stay with this fantasy until you can picture yourself happy and content in your dream home and you've written a couple of paragraphs that make you feel inspired to achieve.

Your work

What kind of work do you want to do? Quite possibly it's a question you've never been asked before as careers advice is something very few of us receive. So many people end up in jobs through circumstance rather than choice, and, after a couple of years in a particular field, you end up with a bit of experience – and that means you're more likely to stay in that field rather than leave because you can earn more if you stay put.

If you really don't know, or mind, what profession you want to work in, think about the things you do for fun and see if there is a career in a related field you would enjoy. You might have missed the opportunity to become a professional footballer, but maybe you could be a groundskeeper at a stadium, a physiotherapist, a bookie, a sports journalist, or an agent or an administrator for your local club. And if you already have valuable skills from your career, think about how you could use them in a field you're more suited to. Football clubs need accountants, cleaners, caterers and maintenance staff as well as strikers and defenders. Make a list of all the things you do for fun, and then ask yourself what jobs you could do in that field that would give you a sense of satisfaction.

Even if you went into a profession you were keen on, possibly even studied for, you may have got sidelined or become disillusioned over the years and your enthusiasm for the profession has been lost. So in this section I want you to imagine your ideal role, the kind of job that would make you excited to get up in the morning and make a difference. These are the kinds of things I want you to think about:

- *What do you want to wear to work?*
  A pinstripe suit? Flip-flops? A uniform?

- *Who do you want to work for?*
  A big corporation? A local firm? Yourself?

- *What kind of place do you want to work in?*
  A corporate HQ? A local factory? Your garden shed?
  Outdoors?

- *Who do you want to work with?*
  Do you work best as part of a team, as the leader of a team,
  or on your own?

Hopefully you're starting to build up a picture of your ideal career. Of course, most people work for money, but a satisfying career isn't just about earning a big salary. Take a careful look at this next list and think about how strongly you agree or disagree with each of the statements. I want you to award a total of fifteen points. You can give all fifteen to one statement if you agree with it particularly strongly, and you do not have to give any points to a statement you disagree with, but you must allocate all fifteen points in total. You cannot use fractions.

POINTS

I want to earn enough money to live on   _____

I want to earn the kind of salary that
lets me buy a few treats   _____

I want a fantastic salary that means I
can buy whatever I want   _____

Flexible hours are really important to me   _____

Job security is really important to me   _____

As long as I enjoy the company of good
colleagues, I am happy at work   _____

I get a kick out of having a job with power   _____

I get a kick out of having an impressive job title   _____

I need to feel I am making a difference in people's lives ___

I want the chance to be creative ___

TOTAL **15**

Most people I've given this test to find there are one or two statements that use up the bulk of their points, with another three or four picking up a couple of points each. I hope your scores have helped you identify what you really want from a career and that you can now picture yourself doing a job that inspires and satisfies you.

Your family

Obviously I don't know what your current family situation is, but for the purposes of this exercise I'm going to assume that, whatever your situation, you want your family to be happy and healthy. This part of the exercise is about working out how the choices you make can in turn make a difference in your family's life.

Think about the people closest to you and ask yourself what you would like to be able to do for them. Put a roof over their heads? Take them on holiday? Send them to a better school? Identify your responsibilities to them and ask yourself this: if you couldn't meet those responsibilities, how would you feel? And if you could provide your family with everything they needed and wanted, how would that make you feel?

Your answers to these basic questions are going to be influenced by whether or not you are financially responsible for members of your family, how big your family is and how much you like them! The thing to remember is that this exercise is about uncovering your hidden goals, and for a lot of people the thing that drives them is making their parents proud, or making their children happy or giving their partner security. Spend a little bit of time thinking how much it would mean to you to be able to do these kinds of things for the people you care about.

If you're young, give some thought to whether or not you want children, and, if you do, think about how many children you would like to have. Picture yourself at some point in the future and try and imagine what sort of family you have. How does that make you feel? For some people, starting and raising a family is the only thing that really matters. Are you one of them? Add these thoughts to the couple of paragraphs you've already written about your dreams for your work and home life.

■ Brits watch an average of 3.7 hours of TV a day. That's more than a day a week spent in front of the box. Imagine what you could do if you gave up TV for a while. *Thinkbox, January 2009*

Love

I've heard a lot of very successful people say they would gladly trade some – or occasionally all – of their professional success for a successful relationship. Some people don't need to be in a relationship to be happy, and there are many people in unhappy relationships, but as it is such an important part of most people's idea of happiness, I think it's sensible to include relationships in this exercise.

Your thoughts will be coloured by whether or not you are currently in a relationship and whether or not you intend that relationship to continue, but don't let your current situation cloud your thinking as you consider the following statements. This time, you've only got three points to award. You can give them all to the statement you agree most strongly with, or split them equally between three statements, or divide them between two statements.

	POINTS
Being in a relationship is vital to my happiness	____
I would rather be single than in a bad relationship	____
I would rather have a successful relationship than a successful career	____
A successful career is my priority	____
I am quite happy on my own	____
I think I would live to regret it if I did not have a successful relationship	____
I cannot imagine going through life on my own	____
TOTAL	**3**

It should be quite obvious from the statements you have chosen how important a long-term relationship is to you at the moment and how motivated you would be to find and maintain one. Over time, your ambitions for your private life will almost certainly change, but your choices here reveal what's currently motivating you. Spend a few minutes now writing down what's important to you at the moment.

Your friends

For some people, the best indicator of success is not how nice a car they have or what job title they've got, it's how many friends they have. The success of sites like Facebook tell me that a lot of people are very motivated by adding to their list of friends and then telling as many people as possible about their activities and achievements. There have been numerous studies over the years that show what a massive impact our peer group has on our attitudes and ambitions. Successful people tend to be friends with other successful people, yet our friends are often our biggest rivals. Someone very witty and clever (and it wasn't one of the Dragons!) said that 'every time my friends are successful a little piece of me dies'. Most friendships have an element of rivalry, and some people use this as a spur to achieve more. A wise woman (it was actually Lowri Turner) once told me that the best form of revenge is success: if you are happy and successful, then your enemies (or your friends!) will be defeated. Don't underestimate how much these small rivalries can effect big changes.

This next test is about discovering just how important your friends are to you so you can find out if they motivate or demotivate you. Take a look at the following pairs of statements. You have to award three points to each pair, and you can divide the points any way you like: 3-0, 2-1 or 1-2. You might find it quite hard to decide which of the statements you agree with the most, and that's why the choice you make is revealing.

POINTS

A I want to be more successful than my friends   ____

B I want my friends to think I am successful   ____

A I want my friends to admire me   ____

B I want to admire my friends   ____

A I sometimes feel jealous when my friends are successful   ____

B I am happy for my friends when they become successful   ____

TOTAL FOR As   ____

TOTAL FOR Bs   ____

If your total for As is higher than your total for Bs, then you are likely to be quite highly motivated by issues about status.

This is not uncommon: although it's not very British to say that we like having the opportunity to brag, the truth is that a lot of us do. Recognising this can help you formulate the kinds of goals that will inspire you to achieve them.

Money

How important a motivating factor is money to you? We all need it, but how much do you *want* it? Ask yourself if you tend to admire people who have money. Would you admire them less if you found out they had inherited their wealth or won it on the Lottery or stolen it?

There's no doubt that having money is better than not having it, but, once your daily needs have been met, how much of your time are you willing to spend trying to get your hands on more of it? Take a look at the following statements. If you agree strongly with the statement, give it five points, if you really disagree with it, give it a zero.

POINTS

I am prepared to work very hard to
    become very rich   ____

I would rather earn more money in a job
    I dislike than earn less money in a job I enjoy   ____

I admire people who have money   ____

I don't care how I earn money, so long as the
    financial rewards are big enough   ____

Becoming a millionaire would make me happy   ____

There is no such thing as too much money   ____

TOTAL   ____

If you scored 25–30 points you are highly motivated by money; in fact, if you scored over 20 points you would probably take the opportunity to stockpile cash whenever you get the chance. If your score is between 10 and 20, I'm going to guess that, as long as your basic needs are met, the thought of earning more money is not much of a motivator for you. If you scored less than 10, you are either already a millionaire or you know that you would rather spend your time in pursuit of different goals. Write down a few sentences that sum up your financial ambitions.

■ The average commute of workers in the UK, France, Germany, Italy and Spain is 35 minutes each way. That works out at 280 hours a year, or 11.6 days. *Business Week, May 2009*

Passion

Let's imagine that all your chores are done, everyone you care about is happy doing activities without you and you have enough money in the bank to take a break. You find yourself with a spare hour or two. What would you do with that time? Now let's imagine that your boss comes up to you and says, 'Do you realise that you haven't taken all your annual leave? If you don't take two weeks' holiday by the end of the month, you'll lose it.' What would you do with that fortnight?

For some, answering those questions will have been easy because they have a passion that drives them. I know very able and highly qualified professionals who have shunned a high-flying career for the safety of middle management just so that they can be sure they will be able to leave the office on the dot at 5.00 p.m. Why? Because they need to feed their passion. Perhaps they live to windsurf, or live to paint or make music; whatever it is, there is something in their life that they feel they cannot live without.

I believe that most of us have a passion, something that we really want to do, but because life gets filled up with everyday activities we often lose touch with the thing we really want to be doing if only we had the chance. So I want you to think about all the things you would like to do with your life if money was no object. Did you have a childhood ambition to write a book? Do you want to cross the Himalayas? Think about all the things you will regret not doing with your life and then write them down.

The next step

By now you should have a few paragraphs written down on each of these subjects – home, work, love, family, friends, money and passion. Now I want you to reduce those paragraphs down into just a few words, the key components in each section that sum up how you feel about these different areas of your life, and write them on the next page:

Home

Work

Love

Family

Friends

Money

Passion

When you've done that, and you can see each of these areas at a glance, I want you to create a mental picture for each of them, turning the sections into an imaginary photo album with images of your ideal home, your perfect job, relationship etc. I want you to really think about what it would mean to achieve the success you are imagining in each of the categories.

And now for the hard part: I want you to tear up six of those photos. If you could only achieve success in one of these areas, which would it be? I did say one of the key factors in being smart with your time was decision-making, so which means more to you than all the others? Be completely honest with yourself – only you will know your answer – and identify the goal that inspires you above all the others and would give you the greatest satisfaction if you achieved it.

It's not easy choosing between goals, but neither is it easy being successful in seven different areas at once! The point of this exercise is to help you uncover your heart's desire so that, as you work through the rest of this book, you will be able to decide how best to allocate your time. However, it's worth noting that if you had done this exercise a year ago, or if you repeat it a year from now, it's entirely possible that your ultimate goal will have changed. Goals can stay the same for decades at a time, but they usually ebb and flow with events and circumstance, and when they do, your motivation suffers and you become less efficient and less effective. If you're ever struggling to work out why you're not getting things done fast enough, ask yourself if the task in hand is taking you towards or away from your goal. You can probably already guess the answer. Identifying and working towards a goal that inspires you is the best way to ensure that you're not wasting your time.

 CHECKLIST

✔ **Identifying your goals inspires you to work more efficiently**

✔ **It's difficult to be successful in several areas at once**

✔ **Our goals change over time: constantly evaluating what we really want helps to motivate us**

2
What are you waiting for?

So now you know what you really, really want out of life, what's stopping you going out and making it happen? What's happening in your life to keep you from the things you really want to be doing and making you waste time on projects and people that don't fulfil you? What are you spending your life doing that you really shouldn't be doing?

I do quite a lot of public speaking at events for entrepreneurs, and people often come up to me and say, 'Hi, do you remember me from last year's event?' Sometimes they have been going to these kinds of seminars for a decade. And at book signings, people will tell me that they really enjoyed my previous books, all of which are based on my life in business. Clearly there are a lot of people out there who *intend* to start a business, but just never get round to it. These days I also meet people who say, 'I'd like to write a book too', and I always encourage them to give it a go, but I know that very few of them ever will. I bet that successful people in all walks of life meet people who say to them 'I'd like to do that too, but . . .' This chapter is about dealing with that little, yet absolutely massive, word – but.

People are constantly making excuses for not getting on with the one thing that they know they really want, or really ought, to be getting on with. The most common reason I hear is 'I haven't got the time'. If that's your excuse, then you're in luck, because the rest of this book is about finding the time and using it more effectively. In the meantime this chapter is about all the other excuses.

I recently heard a story from a friend of mine who had gone to the leaving party for a colleague. His former co-worker was moving to Belize and at the party he asked her what was causing her to make such a dramatic move.

'I want to write,' she answered.

To which my friend thought: 'Couldn't you just pick up a pencil?'

When pressed, she said that she needed peace and quiet to write (which I can understand) and to be free from stress (which also makes sense), and because she wasn't likely to earn much money for a while (that part's definitely true), she needed to move somewhere cheaper. To which my friend thought: 'You can buy a pencil for 10p.'

This woman had put up so many barriers between her and her dream that she had concluded that the only way she could write was to move her entire life to Belize! When I think of the effort, and time, she must have put into that decision – selling her house, researching foreign countries, planning her finances – I can't help but wonder if her writing would have been a better outlet for her creativity and tenacity. I also wonder if, once she got to Belize, she got distracted with renovating her house, or learning Spanish, or establishing herself in her new community and *still* didn't get round to writing. However, to her credit at least she was finally doing something about her desire to write when thousands more do nothing but dream. But she could still just have picked up a pencil. Or bought a laptop and sat at her kitchen table for an hour every night instead of watching TV. By the time she'd settled into her new life in Belize she could have finished her book.

■ 10% of British commuters spend more than 2 hours a day travelling to and from work. For full-time workers, that's about three and a half days a month! *Centre for Transport & Society in the University of the West of England*

The barriers people put between themselves and their goals are often huge, but more often than not they are also imaginary. I've heard people tell me countless times that they intend to start a business 'when their kids are older' or 'when they get made redundant' or 'when they've got a bit more money behind them'. Sometimes people tell me they can't start a business until they've had more experience, yet the most relevant experience they could get is the experience of starting a business!

I can understand that these reservations seem quite reasonable, but further examination usually reveals them to be flawed at best and damaging at worst. Whether you want to write books, start a business or hitch-hike round the world, you could do all of those things tomorrow. If you really wanted to. And you could actively start planning all those things right now.

It's very easy to think that the solutions to your frustrations lie elsewhere and that someone else has the answers. In most cases, there is very little to be gained from waiting and much to be gained from getting on with things straight away. If you wait to do something, the opportunity may fade away; if you wait till you have more money to start a venture you may not be as hungry to make it a success: for almost every excuse I've heard for people delaying their dreams, I always find there is an opposing – and equally plausible – answer.

I think there are three *real* reasons why people don't get on with the things they say they want to get on with. Firstly, they're scared. Scared of failure, scared of looking like a fool, scared of getting hurt. This is perfectly reasonable, but if that sounds like you, ask yourself if it is also perfectly reasonable that you should squander the next few years pursuing something you don't really care about. The second reason is that, frankly, some people are lazy and, unless they're really uncomfortable in their current position, nothing will make them take action to change anything. The third reason is that they don't really want it. For whatever reason, they haven't properly identified and connected with their goals and are paying lip service to something they don't really believe in.

This is why I've started this book spending time to help you find out what you really want to do with your life. Unless you are honest with yourself, you are going to find it hard to prioritise tasks and are not going to be sufficiently motivated to streamline your life and become more efficient, and more successful.

If you really don't know what you want out of life – and as a former beach bum I completely understand if that's the stage you're at – think about what you want to achieve in the next year. Or what you would like to have got done by your next significant birthday. The more time you spend now identifying the goals and ambitions that will inspire you, the more time you will save in the near future.

 CHECKLIST

✔ **Far too many people put barriers between them and their dreams**

✔ **The excuses people make for not getting on with their dreams are almost always flawed**

✔ **The real reasons why people don't pursue their dreams are fear and laziness**

3
What's stopping you?

Once you know what your goals are, good time management becomes a lot easier. All you have to do from now on is ask yourself one simple question about everything you do:

Does this activity take me closer to or away from my goals?

If you are doing something that takes you towards your goals, brilliant. If not, then this chapter's for you.

Life is full of stuff we have to do (like making dental appointments), stuff we should do (like the ironing) and things we want to do (like going to the pub). It is remarkably easy to fill up a day, a week and even a year with things you haven't given much thought as to whether or not it is worth doing them.

I have no problem with people who spend their entire lives in the pub, so long as they have made a conscious decision to spend their lives in the pub. If they have been through a process of evaluation and decided there is nothing better for them to do with their time, that's great. But when they then come up to me and tell me that they would have started a really great business if only they'd got round to it, I think they're wasting my time as well as their own.

This chapter is about consciously evaluating all the activities that make up your day and enabling you to assess whether they constitute a good use of your time. Basically, you're going to need to come up with the answer to one straightforward question: *is it worth it?*

For me, there are plenty of good reasons that make doing anything 'worth it':

List A

I'm getting paid for it.

It's good for my profile.

I'm making useful contacts that will help my career.

I have to do it.

I enjoy it.

It's good for me.

I want to do it.

When I decide if something is worth my time, I juggle these factors. Yet the reasons why we often do things are a bit more like this:

List B

I was asked to do it.

I've always done it.

It's easy.

I feel obliged to do it.

■ The average Briton spends 22 hours 20 minutes online a month. Nearly three of those hours are spent on Facebook.

Nielsen Online, 2009

EXERCISE 2

This simple exercise has three parts to it. All you need is a pen, a sheet of paper and your diary.

PART 1

Start off by identifying the things you are doing for the wrong reasons. Your diary will help remind you of what you've been up to lately. Make two columns on the sheet of paper, one for the activities that you are positively choosing to participate in – the 'good' column – and the other for the things you just happen to fall into – the 'bad' column. If you're doing something for one of the reasons on List A, it goes in the first column; anything else gets put into the other column.

Look at the past three months' entries in your diary and ask yourself why you took part in each activity. You might be going to Pilates classes twice a week and think that this should go in the 'good' column because (a) you choose to go, and (b) it's good for you, but if your teacher isn't much good and you're not feeling any benefit, maybe it should go in the 'bad' column and the hours you save not going to Pilates next week can be spent looking for a better Pilates teacher.

No matter what line of work you are in, there will be events and meetings you need to 'show your face at' to raise and maintain your profile within your industry. Some of these might be tedious, but if they help to make sure that people don't forget who you are, then they're worth attending. I want you really to evaluate everything you do and carefully assess which column the activity should go in. Look at every entry in your diary and ask yourself 'was it worth it?' If the answer's yes, then it goes in the first column, and if it's no, it gets put in the second. Add up the hours you have spent on each.

PART 2

The next step is to look more closely at the 'bad' column and see how many of those activities you can ditch to free up time to spend on the things that matter. If you can, try and work out how many hours you have spent on these activities in the past three months and add up the total.

I think it's unreasonable to think that you can eliminate the 'bad' column altogether as there are certain things you're going to find it hard to avoid, like supermarkets, but you might be able to work out how to spend less time on these activities. So long as by the end of this exercise you are making a conscious decision to go to the supermarket rather than get your shopping delivered, that's OK. Now add up the hours you think you will spend on these activities in the next three months. Hopefully there's a sizeable difference from the total you calculated in Part 1 of this exercise.

As you work through the book, there will be lots of suggestions for ways to minimise the time you spend on tedious activities, so put this list somewhere handy as it will be good to keep coming back to it: by the time you've finished the book, the hours spent on these activities should have been slashed.

PART 3

Now for the hard bit. I want you to look really, really closely at the 'good' column, the list of activities you've been doing because you get a real benefit from doing them. For each entry I want you to identify why you're doing it using the reasons from List A. Next to each entry, write the number that corresponds to the reason in List A. Some activities have multiple benefits – e.g. you're being paid well to do them *and* you enjoy them – so write down as many numbers after the entry as necessary. Now add up how many activities you are doing for money, how many for the profile or status, how many for the future benefits they might bring, how many because you have to and so on.

Is there one category that dominates? Are you mostly doing things for money, or for fun, or because you've got no choice? A productive and effective person will have a good spread of reasons for doing the things they do. If you're doing too much for the money, or too much for the thrill of it, or for any of the other reasons, then I would suggest your time might be better spent if you had a wider spread of benefits. After all, there's no point doing everything for the money if you're not spending some time on securing future benefits from boosting your profile and making contacts: eventually the flow of money will stop if you do that. Odd as it may sound, you can have too much of a good thing: unless you balance the reasons why you do things, you'll lose the ability to be effective and the time you've spent on these activities will have been squandered. Being smart with your time is about making sure you are getting something in return for it. After a while, if you spend too much time on a single activity, you get into the territory of diminishing returns.

Any commitments or activities that take you away from your goals are distractions and if you don't find a way of reducing the time you spend on them, you are reducing your chances of attaining your goals. As you work through the book, you will find suggestions for ways of saying 'no' to distractions and hints on how to find your focus so that you can get the best possible return on the time you invest in anything you say 'yes' to.

CHECKLIST

✔ Life is so full of things we have to do, things we should do and things we want to do, that we forget to work out if it is worth doing in the first place

✔ Asking yourself 'is this worth it?' stops you wasting time on pointless activities

✔ Use your diary to critically assess how much of your time has been squandered on distractions in the past

4
Focus, focus, focus

Now that you've identified your goals, I want to start introducing the skills that will ensure you will achieve your aims in the shortest possible time. The most important of these skills is undoubtedly the ability to focus on the things that really matter and it's one of three core skills I highlighted in the introduction. I can't stress how important this is – if you can eliminate the clutter from your life, you will be able to devote yourself to achieving your goals.

■ American women spend an hour a day longer than American men doing household chores. *American Time Use Survey, 2003*

EXERCISE 3 – Spring-clean your diary

Take a moment to make a list of all the things you have to do in the next week (you could also do this for the next month, and the next year when you've finished this exercise). Write down everything, from doing the laundry to important tasks at work to your leisure activities, and next to each activity write down an estimate of how long you think you will spend on each activity. Once you've finished, look at the list and ask yourself how many of the activities on your list will help you directly reach your goals? I suspect very few. Being smart with your time means reducing the time you spend on the insignificant activities.

Now make three columns with the headings GOALS, UNAVOIDABLE and AVOIDABLE and put each item on your list into one of the columns depending on whether the activity moves you towards your goals, whether or not the task is something you absolutely have to do, or whether it is the kind of avoidable activity you have taken on without giving too much thought to.

The next thing to do is to scrutinise the Unavoidable column and see how many of those tasks can be moved into the Avoidable column if you delegate them to someone else (see Chapter 10 on Delegation, on p. 51). What are you doing with your time that somebody else could be doing for you? Once you've done that, take a closer look at the tasks in your Avoidable column and ask yourself the following questions:

- **Why am I doing this?**
- **Why did I agree to do this?**
- **How can I avoid spending time on this in the future?**
- **Do I really need to do this?**
- **Do I enjoy doing this?**

If you can identify why these tasks have crept into your life and how you can eliminate them from your future, you can devote the time you would have wasted on them to tasks and activities that get you where you want to be. Go back to the list you made a few paragraphs ago and take a look at how much time you had allocated to the tasks you have now identified you do not need to do. Now think how much more you will be able to achieve by spending this time on the tasks in your Goals column.

The last question of the five in the list above is the trickiest to deal with. There's nothing wrong with doing something just for the sheer enjoyment of doing it: I wouldn't advocate removing all pleasure from your life, but spending too much time on activities that take you away from your goals guarantees a life of dissatisfaction. The way to assess how many of these activities you should cut down is by asking another question . . .

What do you want to achieve today?

I was giving some advice to a new entrepreneur who was trying to get more out of his staff. He had delegated tasks to his team and was doing a good job of resisting the urge to meddle in their work, but he wanted to find a way of monitoring their progress without making them feel he was interfering – after all, they had their deadlines and their targets and he had told them it was up to them how they met them.

He had a small team, so he decided that a good way to keep in touch was simply to walk round everyone's desk each morning and ask them what they had on that day and if he could help with anything. I told him that instead of asking his team 'What are you doing today?' the best way to focus their activities was to ask a slightly different question: 'What do you want to achieve today?' When he started doing this, his staff told him different things, he was able to target the help he offered more specifically and the team started to achieve significantly more in the same space of time.

If you ask yourself this question – and it can be adapted to become 'What do you want to achieve this week, or this month, or before your fortieth birthday?' – you can assess if you are focusing too much of your time on avoidable activities, even if they do give you pleasure in the short term.

Staying focused

Once you have identified the things you need to be concentrating on, it's still pretty easy to be blown off course on to time-wasting activities. If you find it hard to stay focused, there are a couple of things you can try that will help.

STEP ONE – Ring-fence tasks

There's quite a well-known saying that goes something like this: a task grows to fill the time available. Which basically means that if you've got half an hour to do something, it will take half an hour, but if you've got an hour, the same task will take an hour. I've already asked you to estimate how long it will take you to do a task; now I want you to imagine that your estimate has become a target. If you have estimated something will take twenty minutes, that is now your deadline for completing the task. At the end of twenty minutes, you must move on to the next task and come back to the first task only when all others have been completed.

If you're estimating how long tasks you don't do very often will take, there's a good chance you will not be all that accurate, but when you are dealing with everyday tasks, your estimates should be pretty accurate. The more you do something, the stricter you should be with your estimates. Over the next few weeks, make a note if you overrun, or if you do things faster than you'd anticipated, and adjust future estimates accordingly. If you have already grouped your tasks together, you should be able to say, 'I will spend an hour doing housework', rather than saying you will spend ten minutes doing the washing up, five minutes vacuuming and so on.

This technique is particularly helpful at work as you can demarcate your day: 'I will spend an hour filing, two hours on

Project X, half an hour organising my expenses.' Being strict with your time allocation means you can be sure you will leave on time.

STEP TWO – Ring-fence distractions

To focus on the things that matter, you have to be able to deal swiftly with the things that distract you from your goals and I find the best way to do this is to make the opposite of a 'to do' list. I want you to make a 'not to do' list.

To start, think of the things that usually stop you from doing what you ought to be doing, like dealing with unwanted sales calls, interference from your boss, chatting with colleagues or teenagers demanding a lift to this, that and the other. So the sorts of things that might go on your 'not to do' list are:

I will not answer the phone after 11.00 a.m.

I will not have more than three cups of tea

I will not watch the news and will only check the headlines using the red button instead

I am not going to work on Project Y

I am not going to spend more than half an hour online

I am not going to do anything that isn't on my plan until I have done everything that is on my plan

I am not going to get dragged into conversations about *The X Factor*

The benefit of writing a 'not to do' list is that it forces you to acknowledge the things that really distract you. What you still need to do, however, is manage the distractions as they come at you. My way of dealing with new information throughout the day is to ask four straightforward questions:

1 How urgent is it?
2 If I do this, what will I not be able to do that I have planned to do?
3 Who can I delegate this task to?
4 Can it wait until I have completed the tasks I had planned to do?

When I have those answers I can either:

1 Deal with it straight away
2 Add it to my plan to do when I have finished everything else I had planned to do
3 Delegate it
4 Decide that it is something I should either reject or ignore

■ American men work an average 8-hour day. American women average a 7.1-hour working day. *American Time Use Survey, 2003*

 CHECKLIST

✔ Good time management is about focusing on the tasks that really matter
✔ Delegate or avoid tasks that take your focus away from your goals
✔ Don't ask yourself 'What are you going to do today'; ask yourself 'What are you going to achieve today' to help you focus on the things that really matter
✔ Ring-fencing your tasks – and your distractions – means you can maintain your focus

5
Don't innovate, replicate

One of the reasons I have been successful in several different industries – residential care homes, children's day care, health clubs – is because I know a good thing when I see it. Contrary to the popular belief that every new business needs a Unique Selling Point, my businesses prove that copying someone else's idea can be even more profitable than having an original idea of your own. So often people tell me that they would start a business 'if only they could come up with the right idea': I tell them not to wait for inspiration but to look at successful businesses they know and see how they can improve on them.

Innovation takes time, and there are no guarantees that the project you are working on will be successful. While I have the utmost admiration for people who work patiently on their own for years developing projects and products or working on creative endeavours, if you want to achieve things quickly, you want to avoid innovation. The world needs innovators – where would we be without them? – but this is not a book about originality; it's a book about being smart with your time.

The great thing about replication as a model for success is that it removes a great deal of risk. While the innovators are spending months, even years, getting their project ready, I can be doing something else with my time. And when they launch their idea, I just have to sit and watch and wait for them to discover all the flaws in their idea. And once they have proved that their idea is workable, and profitable, I just have to find a way of offering what they do slightly better, or slightly cheaper, and I can launch a rival with very little risk. Because they have spent all that time on the innovation stage, I don't have to.

I didn't set out to be the kind of serial entrepreneur who adapts existing business ideas, but it turns out it's something I'm good at and it's something I'd encourage anyone to see if they're good at, too. It's not just businesses you can replicate, whatever field you're in; you just need to look at the successful people around – or ahead – of you, and see how you can modify and improve what they do. In the case of businesses, you don't always need to change the offering particularly, just the location (e.g. you see a successful delicatessen in another town and decide to open one where you live).

Replication saves time in just about every walk of life. If you want to be promoted at work, a fast route to getting what you want is replicating the techniques used by the people who have already been promoted. If those are the skills and attributes that are valued by your company, then those are the ones you should set about acquiring, not the left-field talents that no one knows how to value properly. If you see a model in a magazine or a mannequin in a shop wearing an outfit you like, then buy that exact outfit. You could spend hours traipsing round the shops looking for something similar, or you could have those hours for something useful. If your neighbours have just had a patio laid and you like the stone they've used, then ask them where they got it from and the name of the person who laid the patio – why spend time researching something similar or getting quotes for the work to be done when you can get a recommendation from someone you trust? If you want a new washing machine, why spend endless hours comparing one model with another when someone has already done the research for you? Magazines and websites are full of research and recommendations, some of it compiled by experts in their field. I don't feel the need to replicate their research, only their conclusions.

■ American adults spend a daily average of 8.6 hours in bed.

American Time Use Survey, 2003

Some people want to be distinctive, some people get a kick out of the latest gadgets; I'm not one of them. However, I am very happy for those 'early adopters' and trendsetters to do my research and innovation for me. This may mean that I don't have the most original wardrobe in the world, or the coolest gadgets, but this is a compromise I am happy with because the trade-off is that I have more time for the important things in my life. As I said right at the beginning of the book, there are three themes that will keep coming up if you want to manage your time more wisely, and one of them is compromise.

 CHECKLIST

✔ **Innovation is time-consuming and risky**

✔ **Look at successful people you admire and see if you can replicate their success**

✔ **Let 'early adopters' and trendsetters innovate on your behalf. Let them be the ones to find faults and make mistakes**

6
Second best is close to ideal

I finished the last chapter talking about compromise, and this chapter follows on nicely as it's all about compromise. Perfectionism is often a barrier to progress and it can be very, very time-consuming, which is why I'm often very happy with second best. Notice I didn't say I was *always* happy with it, as there are some exceptions I'll come to shortly. When people talk about 'second best' it's usually about '*settling* for second best', but I think what they are really talking about is settling for third or fourth best, because second best is sometimes the most we can hope for.

In business, people often say 'time is money' as the longer it takes you to do something, the more it costs you in salaries and overheads. Therefore there are times in business when it makes sense to do certain tasks slightly less well if it means you can do them a lot more quickly. Let me explain:

Factory A manufactures the finest widgets in the world. It takes them twenty hours to produce each widget that they sell for £100.

Factory B manufactures pretty good widgets. It takes them fifteen hours to produce widgets that they sell for £80.

Factory A's income per hour is £5, Factory B's income per hour is £5.33. Not only that, for every widget they make Factory B has an extra five hours to spend on marketing or other activities that will help them sell more of their widgets.

For every 100 widgets Factory A can sell, Factory B can sell 133 because they are happy to make less than perfect widgets.

Let's look at another example:

Paul and James are both studying for their GCSEs. They are of equal intelligence, have had the same level of teaching and they both revise for four hours a night. All things being equal, it would be expected that they get identical results.

When Paul has spent two hours revising one subject, he moves on to the next. He hasn't grasped everything, but it's enough to pass the exam. James sticks doggedly to each subject until he is sure he understands everything, but runs out of time to revise each subject.

Paul passes ten GCSEs with modest grades. James passes seven with higher grades than James. For the rest of his life, Paul gets to tell employers he has ten GCSEs, James that he has seven.

So often in life, doing things to a slightly lower level produces more impressive results. But it's not always the case, which is why I say I'm not always happy with second best. There is a calculation to be made that weighs up the time spent against the outcome. If you can spend ten hours on a project and get it 95% perfect, or spend ten hours on a project and get it 100% perfect, then I always strive for – and expect from my staff – that 100%. However, if ten hours' work gets me to 95% but it would take another ten hours to get the last 5%, then that's when I think second best is actually ideal.

This is true in almost every area of life and business. One company can spend so long getting their product design perfect that a rival brings a slightly less perfect product on to the market and grabs the customers, so the perfectionist company is left with a better product they can't sell. At home, you might spend several hours a week making your bathroom sink gleam or mowing your lawn with perfect stripes, but no one other than you will be likely to notice. So long as your sink is clean and your lawn isn't overgrown, no one other than you will ever care. That's because we can't see what's in your head. You might have a vision of the perfection that you're striving for, but the rest of us can only see what you show us. When I drive past a house with an immaculate stripy lawn, do you know what I see? Someone with too much time on their hands.

■ Watching TV accounts for half of all leisure activity in America.
American Time Use Survey, 2003

CHECKLIST

✔ **Perfectionism can be too time-consuming**

✔ **You need to weigh up the time spent on a project against the results you will get**

✔ **Things that are important to you are likely to be insignificant to everyone else: don't worry about the last 5% because no one else will**

✔ **Perfectionism is rarely cost-effective**

7
Play to your strengths

Are you a morning person? Or do you come alive at eleven o'clock at night? We all have different ways of working, and this chapter is about examining the way you live and work to find out where your natural strengths and weaknesses lie. Finding out what you do well and doing more of it enables you to achieve your goals more quickly: if you're always fighting your natural tendencies and abilities, you are going to struggle to get things done, and that means one thing – wasting time.

People succeed, and find tasks effortless, when they put themselves in situations that they are naturally adapted to. You might be familiar with the kinds of personality tests that recruiters ask candidates to take part in. In business, you always want to find out that a potential employee fits the role they're being considered for: if you put a born leader into a team where they won't get the chance to show initiative and motivate the people around them, you will have a disruptive and demoralised presence in your team; and if you offer a leadership role to an introvert or someone who can't delegate, then the efficiency of the whole team will suffer. If you can find out where you excel, and where you fall short, you will know where best to direct your future efforts and instead of spending time and energy fighting against your natural tendencies, you will be harnessing them and racing towards your goals. People are successful when they put themselves in places and situations where success comes more easily to them.

EXERCISE 4 – Accentuate the positive

Let's start by making a list of the things you are naturally good at. I want you to write down ten things you can do better than most people you know. They can be related to your work (e.g. I'm really good at selling advertising space to clients in the car industry) or your leisure time (e.g. I'm really good at cooking spaghetti carbonara) or your home life (e.g. I am really good at making sure the bills get paid on time). Coming up with ten things might be difficult for some people, but I am sure that this is because they are modest, not useless! If coming up with ten is going to be easy for you, then I want you to work a little harder and list the ten things you are *best* at. If you're still struggling, ask family and friends for their suggestions for things you do well.

1 _____

2 _____

3 _____

4 _____

5 _____

6

7

8

9

10

Business teaches you that compensating for your weaknesses is just as important as playing to your strengths. For instance, I have learnt over the years that I am impatient, which is why I employ an MD who patiently attends to the details I'm in too much of a hurry to notice. I know an entrepreneur who's never been able to do his own accounts, but because he knew this about himself he employed an accountant from day one and he is now one of the most successful people I know. You can only compensate for your weaknesses if you know what they are, which is why this next section asks you to come up with ten things you know you're bad at. This might be household chores (e.g. doing the washing-up), work-related (e.g. chairing meetings) or to do with your friends (e.g. forgetting to tele-phone people).

1

2

3

4

5

6

7

8

9

10

Now I want you to look at both these lists and see if there are any patterns emerging. For instance, are you good at things that involve other people, or good at things you do by yourself? Are you good at things that involve teamwork, but rubbish at anything to do with money or maths? The more you can work out *why* you are better at some things and worse at others is the quickest way to work out *how* you can become more efficient in other aspects of your life.

Let me give you an example. I am not great at the fine detail of running a business (I can do it, and have done it, but it's not what I'm best at) and am naturally much better suited to the big picture. It's not a huge surprise, then, that as soon as I was able to employ someone to deal with the day-to-day management and my time was freed up to expand the business, the business suddenly started to flourish. It wasn't just that I had an extra couple of hours a day; it was that I was spending those hours finding deals, which was playing to my strengths.

When you spend your time doing something you're just OK at, you get limited results.

Time + Effort = Result

But when you spend your time doing something you're pretty good at, the equation changes, and so do the results:

Time x Effort = Result

You're spending the same amount of time, expending the same amount of effort, but by playing to your strengths you are transforming what you can achieve.

It really is worth looking again at the lists of things you are good at and things you are not so good at – and adding to them if necessary – to find the patterns. For instance, you might realise that you are good at keeping your workspace tidy, but bad at being tidy at home. If you can work out why – the boss will nag you, you're just keeping up with your colleagues, or it's because you have an area for which you are solely responsible – you can see if the lack of one of these factors allows you to be messy at home (no one to nag you, no inspiration for how things might look if you tried, or it's all shared space so why would you clean up something just for others to make it messy?).

We develop habits in different areas of our life, and habits can be so powerful they actually seem like aspects of our personality. We tell ourselves that we're disorganised, but then find an area of our lives in which we're actually very organised. For instance, I've sat with my kids and helped them with their maths homework and they've been convinced that they were rubbish at maths, but as soon as I've got them to use maths for something practical – like measuring up for a new bit of furniture for their bedroom – they've been brilliant at maths. Another example is an employee of mine who finds it very difficult to concentrate in a noisy office, but when the meeting room is free and she can work in there, she produces spectacular results.

If you can work out why you can do something in one situation (perhaps you are a morning person) and not in another (you are not an evening person) then you can start to play to your strengths.

And as well as learning about what you're good at, you can also learn from what other people are good at. Think of someone in your life who you admire. What do they do well? What is it that they do that you don't? If you can (a) identify what that is, and (b) work out why, then you can really maximise your effectiveness and get more done in less time. Is someone a better timekeeper just because they have mastered the calendar function on their mobile phone? If so, you could teach yourself the calendar function on your phone. Are they a faster worker because they don't get distracted by office chitchat? If so, work out how you could be less distracted by it (use headphones, move your desk, communicate clearly to the people who are talking to you that you don't have the time). If it's not obvious why you're not achieving as much as they are in the same space of time, ask them what they think the secrets of their success are. Tell them that you admire them and ask them for advice and suggestions. People usually like to help, so unless they are highly competitive the chances are that you can get a masterclass for free. Although if you offer to do a favour in return for their advice, you might discover even more. Copying the habits of the effective people you know is a great way of increasing your own productivity.

■ Half of Britons say they spend three or more hours online every day. *Survey for Orange Broadband, 2007*

 CHECKLIST

✔ Write down ten things you are good at, and ten things you are bad at, and see if there is a pattern to your lists. Working out why you are better at some things and worse at others can help you spend your time more efficiently

✔ When you spend time on activities you are good at, you can achieve a lot more in the same time frame

✔ What successful habits and behaviours can you copy from people you admire?

8
Momentum

One of the best ways I know of getting more done in a shorter space of time is to go with the flow. If you're always swimming against the tide, your progress is going to be a lot slower, but if you let yourself be carried along by the tide, you almost get a free ride. Learning to spot and use the momentum of the events and trends that surround you enables you to achieve more in less time.

All sorts of things have momentum. Speak to anyone who's started a business and they'll tell you that, pretty soon after they launched it, the business seemed to have a momentum of its own that the founders weren't completely in control of. Speak to anyone in the music industry, and they'll tell you that it's much easier to get a deal if you are a young, female singer-songwriter in the year that young, female singer-songwriters are considered the hot trend. Speak to authors and they'll most likely tell you that getting started on a new book can take time, but once they're into their stride they write a lot more quickly. In public life, certain ideas slowly gain support until it seems there is a groundswell of opinion that forces the idea into the wider public arena. If you can hitch your cart to the hot new pony, you can get a lot more done a lot more quickly. Whatever line of work you're in, or hope to be in, there are forces all around you that can take you where you want to be.

Identifying momentum

Every industry, every city, every business has its own natural rhythms, and if you can spot them you can work out how you can use them. The kinds of forces at play in industries can be controlled by new legislation that opens up new markets and closes existing ones; some are generated by innovations that change how the industry operates. In the car industry, for instance, the rising cost of fuel and increased awareness of global warming mean customers are increasingly interested in buying 'greener' cars. Any car manufacturer who can design cars that cater to this trend is likely to get more customers more quickly than a manufacturer who ignores this trend. Not only that, but if people who work in the industry can see that one manufacturer is producing more innovative cars, they are more likely to attract the kind of staff who want to work for a forward-thinking company, which in turn means the company can continue to innovate and attract more and more customers. The process has acquired its own momentum, and if the management team of the manufacturer can harness that momentum, then their business will take off. In the same space of time, two companies that started off with near identical profiles can end up with radically different fortunes because one of them didn't spot the right trends.

If we look away from business for a moment and consider urban development, a piece of legislation may designate a certain area as a development zone and encourage architects and construction firms to plan buildings for the area. Once the big projects have been signed off, smaller housing developments usually follow, and when the population is big enough the shops and businesses that will cater for the new population arrive without the incentive from the government that the original developers were tempted by. Eventually, the land around the original development zone might attract investment as the area becomes more desirable. As the momentum has built up, so have the opportunities for people to benefit, either by buying property early or by starting a business that appeals to the incomers. There are times in every cycle when those people who are on the inside can't help but make progress, and, indeed, money.

Within companies there are often periods of rapid expansion that might coincide with rising prices, a new and energetic CEO or technological improvements. Look at your town, your industry and your company and ask yourself what the trends are. Where is the momentum headed?

You can also find momentum in the wider economy and, perhaps more importantly, in your life. Everyone's life goes through different phases, and whether you are studying, working hard at your career, raising a family or about to retire, you will have certain skills that you use and hone at one point in your life that fade when your life is in a different phase. If you're in a phase where the skills you are using and improving also happen to be the skills that are in demand elsewhere in the economy, then there's a chance your career will pick up momentum and you will benefit. If, however, you are focused on raising your family or studying for different skills, you might miss out on that momentum.

Using momentum

It's not much good identifying the momentum if you can't work out how to use it. So once you've spotted the trends and forces that are shaping your industry and your town, you need to see how you can align yourself with the trends and make quicker progress. It might be something as simple as getting trained in a new piece of software that allows you to take on more work.

■ The average office worker loses 48 minutes a day to technological failures, e.g. printers jamming and computers crashing. In addition, they lose an additional 2 hours a day in pointless meetings, dealing with unnecessary phone calls and staving off annoying colleagues. That's nearly 3 hours a day, or around 40% of the working day.

Efficiency in Business Survey, 2005

Once you've caught the wave, you need to stay on it to get the maximum benefit. If you're doing something right, you might as well keep doing it. I've met a few people over the years whose careers were going really well but who were also thinking about setting up a business. They were finding it tough to decide if they should leave a job with prospects for a new, risky venture. So I asked them where the momentum was: were they likely to do very well in their jobs in the near future, or was their new business going to be in a booming area that was picking up momentum? If they could answer that question, I told them they had the answer they were looking for.

If you learn to use momentum to speed up your progress you will stop being the kind of person who uses the excuse that 'the day just ran away from me' for not getting things done. Instead, you'll be the kind of person who runs away with the day.

CHECKLIST

✔ **Things happen more quickly if you can go with the flow**

✔ **Every industry, every city, every business has its own natural rhythms, and if you can spot them you can work out how you can use them**

✔ **Once you've spotted the trends, you need to align yourself with them**

9
The last fiver

There are some people who will do anything to save £5. They will trawl countless websites looking for the lowest possible price on everything; they will even endlessly trawl shops refusing to buy whatever it is they are looking for until they have checked the price in every single outlet. Some people will also negotiate with staff in shops to try and get them to knock a fiver off the asking price, even if it takes half an hour. Like most people, I like getting everything I buy at a good price, but I am not obsessed about getting everything at the best possible price because my time is usually more valuable than my money.

I know that the lowest price doesn't always mean the best deal for my business. If I can deal with a company I trust who can do what I ask by a deadline I've set, that's almost always more valuable to me than dealing with an untried company who can't guarantee they'll meet my deadline. Their quote would have to be substantially lower for me to hire them.

In business you often hear people talk about the cash:time ratio. This is because every hour has a price and entrepreneurs and managers are always looking to spend their time wisely. If I pay someone £20 an hour, how much time should they spend negotiating £20 off the price a supplier has quoted? If you can put a price on your time, you can factor this into your deals. A well-timed deal is often more valuable to my business than a lower-priced deal, and it's true in my personal life, too. An obvious example is taking family holidays during the school holidays. It might be cheaper to book flights and hotels during term time, but the upheaval to family life means paying a higher financial price is better for us.

I don't have time to research the latest flat-screen TVs, so I visit a shop I trust and take the advice of the person who serves me. If I think the price is reasonable, I will buy it; if I think the price is too high, I'll write down the make and model and search for it on a price comparison website, find the cheapest and then buy it. But that's it. That's enough research. I've said that ability to make decisions is one of my three fundamentals of time management. So what if you don't end up with the very best television in the world? At least you didn't spend three weeks of your life looking for something with marginally better functionality that costs £5 less. If I spent any more of my time on buying a TV I wouldn't be able to run my businesses, which ultimately means I wouldn't make the money to pay for the TV. Time, as they say, is money.

Which brings me on to a very important question: how much is your time actually worth? Only when you can put a price on your time can you calculate if searching for the lowest possible price is the best possible use of your time. One way of answering the question might be to calculate your hourly rate, so let's start by working out what that is. Firstly, work out how much you earn in a month, then deduct any tax or National Insurance contributions you make, then divide that figure by the number of hours you work. Here's an example:

Gross monthly income	£2000
Tax	£300*
NI	£140*
Net income	£1560
Hours worked	150
Hourly rate	£10.40

* Rough estimate

Before you answer my next question, give it some serious thought. If your hourly rate was £10.40, how long should you spend searching for a deal that saves you £5? Everyone's answer will be different. If you work a fixed number of hours a week and cannot do any overtime, then why not spend your free time comparison shopping or negotiating to get the best price? People who work as many hours as they can manage may take a different view: why spend time saving £5 when you could be earning even more than that? There is no *right* answer to my question, there's only *your* answer.

■ The average British adult spends 23 hours a week on their sofa. If you also sit down at work and while commuting, this amount of inactivity can lead to posture-related health and back problems.
YouGov poll for Virgin Active, 2008

Of course, the way I've worked out the hourly figure is completely arbitrary. A better calculation for working out how much your time is worth could be to divide your net income by the number of free hours you have each month. For this illustration, let's just say that your free hours are the hours when you are not at work, or not asleep. And let's say you work a forty-hour week, sleep eight hours a night and that your net monthly income is the £1560 figure used in the previous example. Obviously, you should do this calculation using your actual income and your actual available hours.

Monthly income	£1560
Number of free hours a month	308
Price of an hour	£4.88

Now, do you think saving a fiver is worth more of your time? The truth is that neither of these calculations matters all that much: they're just devices to help you reach a conclusion about how highly *you* should value *your* time. However, I think the best way to value your time is to ask yourself a really simple question: what else could you be doing with the hours you're spending trying to save a few quid? If the answer is anything that would make you happier, healthier or richer, then it's time to put an end to your bargain-hunting ways.

 CHECKLIST

✔ **The best deal isn't always the cheapest deal**

✔ **Time is often worth more than money**

✔ **Bargain hunting can be very time-consuming and often produces only modest savings**

10
Delegation

One of the reasons I am able to run several businesses, write books, make TV shows and spend a lot of time with my family is that I have learnt how to delegate. It's not just bosses who delegate; you can delegate to your partner, your kids and your friends as well as employees. Delegation requires a certain amount of compromise, one of the key factors that underpins good time management. Delegation means letting go of being a perfectionist, which again brings us back to compromise. When you delegate, things might not be done exactly as you would do them, but (a) that doesn't mean other people can't do things as well as you (or better), and (b) you'll quickly realise that delegation also allows you to focus on the goals that only you can achieve. And, of course, focus is one of the other fundamental concepts of smart time management. That's why delegation is so important: I actually think my ability to delegate is one of the major factors in my success. It's no wonder, really: the best way to get more done yourself is to get other people to do a lot of your work for you!

Why delegate?

Not everyone can be brilliant at everything, which is why a lot more can be achieved if people who are best suited to a task carry it out. There's a reason why businesses have sales departments and accountancy departments: it's because some people are good at selling and some people are good at accounts. Teams can achieve more than individuals and, if you delegate successfully, you are building a team that can propel you forward at speed.

If you are not skilled or confident in a certain area, you will take a long time to complete a task in that field. Someone who is trained or experienced in that area will do the same job in much less time. A great example of this is decorating your home. Most people can pick up a paint brush and decorate a room, but without the right tools and the know-how they will take longer than a professional decorator who will do it in half the time – and probably do a better job. Even if you are extremely capable of carrying out the task you are thinking of delegating, if you can get someone else do carry some of the load you are freed up to do more meaningful or more enjoyable tasks. And there's another benefit, too: let's say you decide to delegate the task of ironing your teenagers' clothes to them; not only do you save time, but you train your kids in a new skill that means you can *always* delegate the ironing of their clothes. Delegation empowers the people around you to do tasks they might otherwise never master. The end result is a well-rounded, multi-skilled team that can achieve a great deal more than one flustered individual can.

If you are working hard, you might be tempted to rush certain tasks and in doing so miss out vital details. Or you might just exhaust yourself so much that you are good for nothing. Delegation is a way of making sure that important jobs get the attention they deserve and that key people are always free to do what needs to be done.

What to delegate

The best tasks to delegate are the ones that you (a) don't enjoy, (b) aren't any good at, and (c) are the ones that other people are great at. An obvious example of something that a lot of people delegate is their accountancy. They aren't familiar enough with the latest tax thresholds, they don't have the knowledge of what exemptions they can claim and they are not familiar with the forms they have to fill in. Preparing their own accounts or completing their own tax return would take them days, they would hate doing it and there would be a reasonable risk that they would make a mistake. It's no wonder that a lot of people would pay an accountant to do this for them.

However, some people often delegate tasks that they would actually quite like to do themselves. The best example here is childcare. I've known many couples over the years who have used a childminder or a nanny when they really wanted to be the ones to raise their kids. They had realised they could not do everything, had looked at all their options and decided to use childcare as a means of getting on with the things that only they could do – like earning money.

There are some tasks – and childminding can be one of them – that are straightforward enough to delegate as there are nanny agencies and registers of childminders; any tasks that can be carried out relatively easily by other people are good candidates for delegation. Where people often go wrong is when they try to delegate tasks that cannot easily be carried out by other people, things that require constant referrals or countless decisions, and that is why people often say 'it would be quicker if I did it myself'.

Who to delegate to

You can delegate tasks to anyone in your life. You can get your partner to pick up a takeaway on his or her way home; you can get your kids to tidy their rooms themselves; you can get your friends to book tickets for the theatre; you can get your local shop to order in goods instead of sourcing them yourself; or get a travel agent to book your holiday for you. You don't have to have staff to find people to share your load.

At work, it's not just the people who report to you that you can delegate tasks to. Your co-workers and even your boss might be the right people to pass on certain duties to. Staff occasionally come to me and ask if I can do something for them so that they can then get a lot more done themselves. Within your team at work there maybe someone who is naturally more suited to certain activities than you are, and a redistribution of tasks may help to make you all more efficient.

How to delegate

The art of delegation is surprisingly simple. Effective delegation involves setting targets and deadlines, empowering the person you are delegating to so that they can do the task with confidence and then letting them get on with the task without interference. Here's how to do this in a bit more detail:

- Agree what each of you is responsible for. Make sure that everyone knows how their task fits into the bigger picture so that you are all working towards the same, or shared, goals. Make it clear how important their role or task is.

- Agree achievable targets with each other, e.g. you will clean the house while your partner cooks before your guests arrive.

- Make sure that whoever you are delegating to has the means to carry out the task you've delegated, e.g. making sure your partner has the skills, the ingredients and the time to produce a meal.

- Set a deadline for reaching those targets. Telling the kids to tidy their room isn't as effective as telling them to tidy their room by 8.00 p.m.

- Let your team know they can come to you if they run into difficulties, but unless what they're doing compromises your ultimate goal, they should be allowed to make their own decisions.

- *Then just let them get on with their work without interference. Checking up on your team not only slows them down, it slows you down, too.*

If you are not used to delegating, this last rule can be difficult to follow. If you are handing over a task that you have done yourself for years, whether it's getting a cleaner or employing an external marketing agency, you will have certain views on how things should be done. The thing about delegation is that 'how' starts to be much less than important than 'when'. So long as the work is done to the specified standard by the specified time, the 'how' matters a lot less.

■ American adults spend 8.5 hours a day, on average, looking at one type of screen or another. That's either their TV, mobile phone, GPS, PDA or computer. *Council for Research Excellence, 2009*

If you find delegation difficult

Delegation is such an important tool because it lets you get more from your time, which is why it really is worth persisting with, even if you find it difficult. The key is to work out why you are finding it difficult. Some people are control freaks, and if you fall into that category it can help to look closely at your attitude. Focus really tightly on the job you want to outsource to someone else, imagine how well you would do it and then imagine how you think someone else would do it. What is the difference between the two pictures? Let's say, for example, that you happen to be particularly concerned that a landscape designer won't lay a new lawn precisely parallel with your house; the simple solution is to tell the landscaper that the lawn has to be precisely parallel or they won't be getting paid. If you can identify your fear, you can ensure that it never comes to pass.

If you've never delegated before, it's understandable to lack confidence in your ability to do it, so why not start by delegating small tasks until you grow in confidence? Try it a few times and learn just how much time you can have to yourself when other people do the work. When you get used to having more time for the things that matter, delegation will become a necessity.

There may be one other reason why you find delegation difficult, and that's because you can't find good people to delegate to. This is a real problem that isn't easily solved, but it is worth taking the time now to find a better childminder, a better accountant, a better secretary or, dare I say it, a better partner, so that in the long term you are surrounded by a team you can trust.

CHECKLIST

✔ Delegation allows skilled specialists to carry out specific tasks with greater speed and efficiency

✔ Delegation helps you build a successful team – whether at work or at home

✔ Tasks can be delegated to friends, family, co-workers, suppliers and even bosses

11
Work with what you've got

One sure way to slow your progress through life is to keep changing direction. If you are always starting afresh, you can't build on the foundations you've made and you will constantly be spending time learning new skills instead of utilising old ones. If you can use what you've already got, you can give yourself a head start. This chapter is about recognising the skills and contacts you already have that can propel you towards the future.

Who do you know?

They say it's not what you know but who you know that counts. There's certainly a lot of truth in that, though I started my first business without any useful contacts. However, I soon surrounded myself with a great team and I was able to make much swifter progress towards my goals, so ask yourself this: who do I know who can help me make progress? If you can identify the people in your life who you can turn to for support, advice and introductions, you can propel yourself towards success. You may think you don't know anyone useful or anyone who could make introductions or offer valuable advice, but I have learnt that we are all much better connected than we think.

You've probably heard of the 'six degrees of separation' theory that suggests everyone on the planet is, at most, six steps removed from everyone else. What that means is that if, say, I wanted to speak to the president of Russia, it would take just five phone calls because someone I know will know someone who knows someone who knows someone else who could put me in touch with Mr President. The trick is knowing the right person to call in the first place, so let's take a closer look at the people in your life and see who can give you a leg up.

I want you to think about everyone you know, not just the influential or successful people, because it's often the people you know less well who turn out to be the most useful. If you think about it, this makes sense as your immediate friends and family tend to know the same people that you know and have similar spheres of knowledge. The people who are a little distant from us who move in different social circles will tend to know different things and different people – exactly the kind of contacts who can help you on the first stage of your journey towards your goal. So as you work through this chapter, keep in mind that your most useful contacts might not be your closest friends: they might be former colleagues, acquaintances, neighbours or just people you know from the gym.

Get out your address book, go through your email contacts, look at your friends on Facebook.com or MySpace.com, see who you went to school with on FriendsReunited.com and ask yourself if any of them could help you get where you want to go. Who could open doors for you or smooth paths? Think about what they do for a living, what their hobbies are or who they might know who could help you make progress.

What do you know?

I'm sure most of us have been at a party and been introduced to someone new and within a few minutes they will have asked you the classic party question: 'So, what do you do?' The problem with this question is that we tend to answer very simply – 'I'm an accountant' or 'I'm a dentist' or 'I'm a builder' – and in doing so I think we undervalue any skills we have that do not directly relate to our professional life. If you are looking to propel yourself towards your goals, you ignore the peripheral knowledge you have acquired at your peril. Just because you don't have a professional qualification in gardening it doesn't mean you couldn't tell Alan Titchmarsh something about petunias; and just because you've never been paid for your DIY it doesn't mean that those skills aren't extremely valuable.

I want to encourage you to exploit everything you know and everything you do and to see all of these as assets as you plot your route to success. In all likelihood, your goals stem from things you are passionate about, and if you are passionate about something you are probably also knowledgeable about it. What do you know that no one else knows? What 'inside' information do you have that can unlock the future?

■ 46% of Britons claim they have less free time than they did three years ago. *Poll for Swiftcover, 2009*

Where do you know?

I have started all my businesses in the part of the north-east of England where I live. When I sold ice creams from an ice-cream van, I knew where the schools and parks were, and therefore where the kids who were my customers would be. When I started my care home business it was because I'd been to see the existing care homes in my area and was appalled at the conditions I saw elderly people living in. And I opened my first health club because the nearest one was more than half an hour's drive away. I was able to exploit my local knowledge to make a successful business: what do you know about your local area that can help you move on in your career, your business or your home life? Where is the opportunity? What do you know about the area that an outsider doesn't? What chances can you seize before somebody else does?

 CHECKLIST

✔ You can make faster progress if you can build on the experience you already have

✔ Constantly changing direction makes it harder to gain momentum

✔ Use the knowledge you have gained through work, leisure and life to spot and exploit opportunities

12
Stop kidding yourself

On **Dragons' Den** I often hear pitches from people who have been working on their business plans for years. Sometimes they have developed new products and secured patents, often at considerable financial cost, but, sadly, it's frequently clear to the Dragons that they've been wasting their time. Over the years, I've come to realise that a form of blindness affects a percentage of the entrepreneurs we meet because some of them just can't see sense. They have spent too much time and too much money on their project to admit that it's just not good enough. Some of them have been holding on to their dream for so long that they cannot let go, and, no matter what the Dragons tell them, we know they're going to go home and keep wasting their time as well as their money.

Imagine you're at a dinner party and you're introduced to a man in his fifties who tells you that he's going to be a pop star. I don't know what you'd say to his face, but I know what you'd be thinking: *he's kidding himself*. If you've ever watched *The X Factor*, then at some point you must have screamed at the screen 'Don't give up the day job' to deluded contestants who think they have a future in the music business. The success of Susan Boyle will no doubt keep many delusional dreams alive. Yet even people who can spot someone who should have given up on their dream ages ago on *Dragons' Den* or *The X Factor* are incapable of recognising when it is they who should be throwing in the towel! Before we get to the end of this chapter, I want to make sure that you're not one of them.

Clearly, I've taken a couple of extreme examples, but I'm sure you know of people in your life who are waiting and hoping for outcomes they are very unlikely to see. Whether they expect to get a job offer beyond their experience or think their married lover will leave their spouse, people squander precious time kidding themselves that miracles happen. Of course, 100-1 shots occasionally win the Grand National, and that's why so many people continue to delude themselves.

But before I go any further, I want to make it clear that I'm not telling you to abandon the goals and dreams you identified in the first chapter; I just want you to start calculating the odds of your success in your chosen field so that *you* can decide if you are kidding yourself and that pursuing your goals is a good use of *your* time. If my kids told me they wanted to be an astronaut or the Prime Minister or a pop star, I wouldn't try and stop them but I would point out how much effort it would take to attain their goals. And then I'd point out all the things that could go wrong and tell them that their chances of achieving their dreams were probably pretty low, even if they worked extremely hard and were extremely talented. And then I'd ask them the really important question: imagine it's ten years from now and you haven't achieved what you set how to achieve. What will you regret more? Not getting what you wanted, or never having tried at all? If failure to succeed would be less painful than the failure to try, they should pursue their dreams; but even then I would probably tell my kids that they should have a back-up plan.

Entrepreneurs often talk about taking risks and the popular perception is that there's no reward without first taking a risk. That's true, but successful entrepreneurs know it's not just about taking a risk; it's about *calculating* the risk in the first place. There's a whole branch of business that's devoted to 'risk management' and big corporations have teams of people assessing the likelihood of certain outcomes and devising contingencies.

That's all I want you to do here: assess the risk that you are kidding yourself, and, if it turns out that there's a chance you might be, then limit your exposure by planning an alternative. We can't avoid risk, but, by doing this, you minimise your exposure to *unnecessary* risk.

I did a bit of acting a few years ago and appeared in a couple of TV shows after going to drama school. The tutors on my course were keen to point out that something like 92% of actors are out of work at any one time, yet everyone on the course thought they stood a chance of being in the other 8 per cent. What I noticed was that the sensible people I met at school and on set all had a trade behind them. I've since met a few footballers who also make sure they have something to fall back on if they get injured and are forced to retire.

There's nothing wrong with trying to achieve your dreams, but you can often do this in conjunction with a back-up plan. If this was a book about starting a business, I might tell you not to bother with a back-up plan as knowing that there's no alternative to making your new business a success can be the kick up the backside that ensures it becomes a success. However, this is a book about being smart with your time, and the nature of risk means that pursuing your dreams can often end in disappointment. You then have to look back at the other chances you missed while you were focusing on a pipe dream, and look around you at people who made duller choices but who have more to show for them.

It's not for me to say which is the right option for you; I only want you to be aware of the possibility that following your dream might be a big waste of your time. However, I should point out that, when I started my first business, I had friends and neighbours telling me it was a pipe dream that would see me broke. I took a big risk starting a business, but it was a risk I was aware of and a choice I was more than happy with.

EXERCISE 5 – **Analysing your goals**

Let's go back to the goals you identified in Chapter 1 and assess the risks you will be taking if you follow them. For each of your goals, I want you to list the following:

What's stopping me from achieving this outcome?

What needs to happen for this goal to be achieved?

How dependent am I on other people to achieve this goal?

How likely is it that I will look back on my time pursuing this goal and wonder what the hell I was doing with my time? How likely is it that if I don't pursue this goal I will kick myself for never really trying?

What you're trying to work out is the likelihood that you will be successful in your chosen aims so you can assess the risk you are taking in pursuing them. You are basically asking yourself how great the chances are that you will be wasting your time.

■ 17% of Britons say they spend too much time checking their email.
Poll for Swiftcover, 2009

If you are not sure if your answers are telling you to quit now or not, perhaps the following might help you reach a conclusion:

Give yourself a deadline

Work out how long you are prepared to follow your dream for. If you put a time limit on a project, you instantly inject a level of enthusiasm to achieve the goal by the stated deadline.

Putting limits around your dreams can actually make them more attainable. You sometimes hear experts say that 'children need boundaries' because they are far more likely to reach those boundaries if they know they are there to be reached. I think the same is true of goals. Give your goal a boundary by giving yourself a time limit. If you haven't reached your goal by the time your limit has been reached, then you have to promise to walk away and spend your time on something more likely to get results.

Look for precedents

The reason why we all think the fifty-something wannabe pop star is wasting his time is because there aren't many examples of pop stars finding fame and success in their fifties. A good way of assessing whether or not you'll be wasting your time is to look for people like you who are already doing it. For instance, if you've been waiting for a promotion in your firm for years, look at the people who have been promoted ahead of you. If you're not like them, if you don't have their skills and attributes, the chances are your firm does not value people like you and you are almost certainly wasting your time working for them if you want to get promoted. The more precedents you can find, the less likely it is that you are wasting your time.

Ask your friends

Share your goals with your friends and family and ask them if they think it is likely that you can achieve your aims. Ask them what they think the barriers to your success might be. Be warned though: there are some people who really don't like the idea of their friends becoming successful, but you can still use their doubts to your advantage. Your cynical friends may spot pitfalls and barriers that you have optimistically ignored.

Identifying potential problems is the first step in overcoming them.

 CHECKLIST

✔ Sometimes people have invested too much in their dream to analyse their real chances of success

✔ Assess your chances of success before you spend too much time on a pipe dream

✔ Only you can decide if you would regret not pursuing your dream more than you would regret failing to make your dream come true

13
Walking away

Everyone reading this book will have different goals. If you asked all your friends to go through the exercises in Chapter 1 to uncover their hidden ambitions, you would find that you all want slightly – or very – different things from life. Ultimately, what that means is that at some point you are going to have to walk the path to your future on your own. At some point – or at several points – your path is going to diverge from that of your friends, colleagues and family. There will come a time when all of us will have to break away from the safety of what we've known to explore somewhere new on our own. Failure to recognise these junctures in your life, and failure to take the right path, means spending chunks of your life on things you don't care about, and those are the kinds of things you are going to look back on and consider a waste of your time. The ability to walk away from the familiar towards the unfamiliar is a key skill in being more productive with your time. The good news is that the very act of making a positive decision can invigorate you, give you a jolt and create momentum that propels you towards your goals.

Calculating if you would be better off if you walked away isn't always easy, not just because the benefits of staying or leaving are finely balanced but because you are often weighing up things you do know against things you don't know for sure. Walking away sometimes means being comfortable with a certain amount of uncertainty, and in these situations it helps to look back at the last time you did something for the first time. Whether or not that was a happy or successful situation, you can learn something about your attitude to change. If you know you find change difficult, then of course you are going to find walking away from certainty hard. If, however, you are a thrill-seeker, you are going to tend towards making rash decisions just because you want to shake things up a bit. Knowing this about yourself can help you make better assessments about your future.

One of the main reasons why people don't walk away from situations sooner is because they don't realise that the moment to make changes has arrived. It's only with hindsight that they see they stayed too long in a situation that was wasting their time. The only way to stop this from happening is to set aside time to regularly assess your progress towards your goals. In my businesses we perform something called a SWOT analysis every three months, and I think that if you do the same, it will help make sure you are always walking in the right direction.

SWOT stands for Strengths, Weaknesses, Opportunities and Threats. Every three months I sit down with my management team and we look at what we're getting right and where we're losing ground, and then we look at the wider industry and economy and anticipate where the opportunities for growth will come from, and assess potential threats to our future prosperity. A formal review could work for you, too, as it ensures that you will never spend too long walking down the wrong path. Taking the time to ask yourself a few key questions can stop you wasting your time on projects, people, careers and investments that are taking you away from your goals. These are the sorts of questions I would suggest you ask yourself:

Are you happy?

If your job, your relationship, your friendships or your domestic life are making you unhappy, ask yourself if this is because you know you are wasting your time and energies on something that really isn't what you want.

Are you bored?

Being bored is a clear sign that it's time to move on. Unless you think the boredom is temporary, I would take this as a wake-up call to make some changes.

Are you dissatisfied?

What are you not getting that you should be getting? How can you make changes to ensure you find satisfaction? If it's not going to come from your current job/career/social scene, then it's time to walk away.

Are you comfortable?

Being comfortable isn't necessarily a bad thing, but being too comfortable can make you lazy and that means that you stop noticing the opportunities for positive change and the threats that bring negative change.

Is it too good to be true?

It's usually true that when something seems too good to be true, it is. In the economy, for example, plenty of people predicted the world was heading for a major recession early in 2007 and moved their investments into safer havens before everyone else realised that the boom wouldn't last forever. If your instincts are telling you that something is too good to be true, it might well be time to take a hike.

When no one else can see what you see

I've already talked about the people I've met through *Dragons' Den* who spend years of their lives on projects that are clearly heading nowhere. If you find yourself in a situation where you are the only one who can see the upside, there's a chance you are kidding yourself and your efforts will bring greater rewards if you redirect them elsewhere.

What's the worst that could happen?

This is a great question to ask yourself when you are trying to work out if now is the right time to take action. What's the worst that could happen if you stay put, and what's the worst that could happen if you take a leap into the unknown? When you do this, staying put can seem a lot scarier than making changes.

■ 13% of Britons say hanging on the phone for people or call centres is the biggest waste of time. *Poll for Swiftcover, 2009*

 CHECKLIST

- ✔ We all want different things out of life, and that means that there are certain paths we are going to have to walk alone
- ✔ Performing a SWOT analysis can tell you when it's time to walk away
- ✔ Working through the questions in this chapter can help you decide if you should stay or if you should go

14
Ignoring the little voice

Since I started public speaking and talking to would-be entrepreneurs about their ventures, I have noticed that many of them hold back from going for their dreams for a reason that isn't often recognised. This single factor makes people dither, it clouds their decision-making and it wastes not just their time, but the time of the people they talk to about their idea. This barrier, this cause of so much time-wasting, is doubt.

Even when friends and family are urging them forwards, even when they have spreadsheets that predict success or market research that suggests people will buy whatever it is they're selling, they have a little voice inside that says: 'Are you sure?' Listening to the little voice makes people wait, and therefore miss opportunities; it makes them hedge their bets and divides their attention; and it can persuade them not to follow their dreams.

It's not possible to live a life without doubt, but it is possible to manage doubt in a way that lets you get on with making things happen. This is how I do it:

1 You're not going to be right all the time

People are often so worried about being wrong that they don't give themselves a chance to be right. If you can accept that you are going to be wrong some of the time, you are liberated to give something a go.

2 Put a time limit on it

If you really can't make your mind up about a decision, one way to move forward is to put a time limit on it. This can work two ways. (1) You could say: 'If I can't make my mind up about it by the end of the week, then it's obviously something I shouldn't do', or, (2) You could say: 'Because I'm not 100% sure about this, I am only going to pursue it for one week/month/year, and if I have not achieved what I had hoped by the end of that time, I will abandon the idea and at least I will have only spent one week/month/year on it.'

3 Put a cash limit on it

Most courses of action involve spending money, and if you are unsure about which path to take, it may be because you are nervous about squandering cash. One way to free yourself up to take a chance is by putting a limit on how much you are willing to spend on your plans. Say to yourself: 'I will put heart and soul into this until I have made a success of it, or spent £100/£1000/£10,000 on it.' It's always a good idea to write that figure down otherwise there is always a possibility that you will let yourself spend an extra amount, and, when that happens, you carry on pursuing something that you would be better walking away from.

4 Put it in a drawer

If you are taking your time to make a decision, the best thing to do might be to ignore the issue in question and, either literally or metaphorically, put it in a drawer. Seriously, write down the thing you're stalling over and put the piece of paper somewhere you can't see it. If it's a case of out of sight, out of mind, then at least you've been getting on with something else; if, however, you can't stop yourself from thinking about the piece of paper in the drawer, then maybe that's telling you to go ahead with your plans.

5 Think about the future

A great way to silence the little voice of doubt is to imagine it's five years in the future. Ask yourself if a future you would tell you to go for it, or to walk away. Even if your plans don't bring the success you hope for, would a future you rather you had given it your best shot, or lived with the regret of never knowing?

6 Not today

I think doubt is a bad habit. I used to have a lot more doubts and hear the little voice a lot more often, but as my career has progressed, I've become much better at making decisions and ignoring the little voice. Years ago, I couldn't quite tell it to go away, but I kept telling it: *not today*. If you can banish doubt for just one day, just to see how things go, you start to move forward. Eventually, of course, my little voice got the message and, as I grew in confidence about my ability to make decisions,

I was less and less held back by doubts. If you want to start somewhere, start with telling the little voice to leave you alone for twenty-four hours.

■ In 1980, the average one-way commute in London was 2.5 miles. In 2003 it was 8.5 miles. *University of the West of England*

 CHECKLIST

✔ **Doubt can stop us making quick and reasonable decisions**

✔ **Accepting that you are not always going to be right frees you up to be decisive**

✔ **Being indecisive is a habit. Breaking the habit can transform your effectiveness**

15
Just say no

reckon there are three reasons why people don't get everything done that they want to get done. Either they are inefficient, they don't have enough time available or they have too much to do in the time available. If you want to improve your effectiveness, you have to work out which of these variables is the cause of your problem. So far I've talked about ways to become more efficient (and there are a lot more in the second half of the book) and suggested ways in which you could create more time in your life (again, there are more suggestions to come). This chapter is about the third reason: having too much to do. Being more efficient can free up a few hours that would otherwise be squandered, but there is always going to be a limit to how much extra time can be found and that means . . .

you can't do everything.

Which in turn means that there are times when you have to say no to new opportunities, as well as goodbye to existing commitments. Having too many commitments ensures that nothing is ever done to the highest standards, you disappoint the people around you and you are in a perpetual state of panic. Having a manageable number of commitments ensures goals are achieved and progress is made. If you feel that you don't have enough time each day, you need to learn to say no.

Existing commitments

Let's start by looking at what already takes up your time. I want you to make two lists. The first list is of everything you regularly find yourself doing outside work, and the other for activities that take up your time at work. Here are some suggestions of activities that might end up on some people's lists:

HOME	WORK
Housework	Paperwork
Shopping	Meetings
Gardening	Email
Paperwork	Research
Reading/cultural activities	Reading reports
Spending time with family	Preparing budgets
Taking kids to activities	Networking
DIY	Responding to emergencies
Charity work	Dealing with clients
Organising community events	Sales
Car maintenance	Promotion and marketing
Keep fit	Forward planning
Socialising	Taking a lunch break
Taking a holiday	Socialising

Notice that on the work list I haven't actually included doing the work you are being paid to do! So much of our time is taken up with thoughtless activities – and by that I mean things we do without thinking – that we can spend entire days (if not longer) on things we did not make a conscious decision to spend time on. If you can eliminate those activities from your life you will have all the time you need to focus on the things that really matter to you.

So let's start with your HOME list and see what we can remove. The first question to ask is if there are any responsibilities that you could delegate to someone else, or activities you could live without doing. What's on that list that you know you will look back on and say 'that was a waste of my time'? What's on the list that you could do less of? Identifying the activities that have been unconsciously filling up your life is the first step in unclogging your life.

If you're the sort of person who sits on committees or volunteers for charities, it's possible you've taken on too many responsibilities. Do you need to do all of them? Can you tell the organisations now that you intend to stand down at the earliest opportunity? If you're a sociable person, you're probably likely to say yes whenever a friend asks you to take part in something, but now's the time to assess whether or not you really ought to be spending your time on activities that someone else chose, rather than you.

Assessing new opportunities

Once you have reduced the number of your commitments, you need a strategy for making sure that you don't start to fill up your days with the same sorts of commitments you've just extricated yourself from! If you're the sort of person who likes to say yes, you need to develop a set of criteria that allow you to be more selective. Asking yourself these questions will help:

- Do I really want to do this?
- What will I *not* be able to do if I spend my time on this?
- How much of my time will it take up?
- Can I reduce my commitment in the future if it gets too much?

- Do I have the time to do this?
- Will I be able to get help if it starts to be too much?
- Am I only saying yes because it's easier than saying no?
- Will I have enough time to do it properly?
- Does this take me towards or away from my goals?

From the answers to these questions, it should be obvious whether the opportunity in front of you is one you should pursue.

It's hard to say no

I have recently had to start turning down invitations to join charities that I know I could be passionately committed to if only I had the time. I now work with twenty-nine charities and the benefit of charity work for me – rather than for the people the charities help – is knowing that I can make a difference. If I said yes to every offer I received, I would cease to make a difference to the charities I supported. I just wouldn't be able to do very much for them, and they would quickly learn that they couldn't rely on me. I have reached my limit, and I recognised that before I took on commitments that I knew I couldn't handle. But it does mean I have had to say no when I have really wanted to say yes.

■ On average, Britons sleep for an extra 43 minutes a day at the weekend. *The UK Time Use Survey, 2000*

Saying no can be hard. I think it's a basic human instinct to want to help and to want to agree with people, which is why I think most people's first response is usually positive. Saying no often means putting yourself first, but if you want to achieve your goals that is what you are going to have to do.

There are, of course, nice ways to say no, and if you know you can say no with grace then maybe you'll find it a little easier to do. Here are my tips:

- Don't just ignore people. They will only keep asking and that may take up more of your time
- Explain why you can't say yes
- Suggest other people they could go to for help
- Be honest: if it really isn't for you, you should say so

 CHECKLIST

✔ Saying no to new opportunities is the only way to make sure you do not take on too many commitments

✔ You might be able to delegate certain tasks to other people

✔ Develop a strategy for assessing new opportunities – that way you won't say yes when you should be saying no

16
Detox your life

Every January magazines fill pages – and TV shows fill hours – telling us all how to detox our diet after the overindulgences of Christmas. We're told that cutting out a few bad foods can give our digestive systems a rest and boost the efficiency of our vital organs. We can get different kinds of benefits if we detox our lives instead of our diets and this chapter is about removing unhelpful – or toxic – activities that clog up our days. We're used to the concept of controlling our diet and exercise if we want to control our weight and our health, and I think we can extend the concept of the diet to time management.

The thing with diets is that they all work in different ways: some tell you only to eat protein, others to only eat fruit and others not to eat anything after 6.00 p.m. – surely they can't all be right? I've come to the conclusion that it's not the science behind the diet that helps people lose weight, it's the structure that the diet imposes on their food intake that helps them monitor what they eat. The same is true for 'time diets': what works for some people may not work for others, but if you can find a diet that works for you, the structure it imposes on your use of time will encourage you to be more efficient and stop you wasting time.

The reasons why diets work (at least in the short term) is that they encourage you to monitor and evaluate your food intake instead of just eating whatever you fancy whenever you fancy it. They give you a structure, or a template, for healthier eating, and it therefore becomes easier to avoid fattening foods while you actively start looking out for healthier foods. A 'time diet' has the same principles: by developing a structure for your time management, you will find it easier to make better choices about what to do with your time. But, just like diets, not every technique will suit everyone: you have to keep trying, or searching, until you find the template that works for you.

So far, we've already identified areas of your life where you are doing things that don't help you achieve what you want to achieve, either because you're too nice to say no, or because you've got into some bad habits. Now is the time to take action. I want you to look at the areas that you've identified as needing to be surgically removed from your life and work out the action to be taken. I'm going to take different areas of your life in turn, and suggest easy ways to make changes that will make a big difference. Make a note of each of the suggestions that would work for you and start to tailor your own personal time diet.

Home life

By now, you should already know what you are spending too much time doing. The question we need to answer now is 'What are you going to do about it?' Are you going to reduce the number, or frequency, of household chores you do, delegate them to someone else in your household or pay someone else to do them? I've always believed that if you have an extra cupboard, you'll find a way of filling it. Can you de-clutter your house and streamline your possessions? Have a good clear out and reduce the number of possessions you have: if you only have a few pairs of shoes you're going to get dressed a lot quicker, and if you only have one place where you file all your paperwork, you'll find documents so much more quickly. There's a great statistic I found from the National Soap and Detergent Association in the US: getting rid of excess clutter would eliminate 40% of housework! Go on – have a clear out!

And it's not just your possessions that can slow you down: have you identified the occasions when other members of your household pull you away from what you *should* be doing? If so, how are you going to respond the next time the kids ask for a lift or your sister asks you to baby-sit? Are you developing your strategy for saying no?

As with food diets, it can be very difficult sticking to your diet when the rest of your household is still behaving the way they always did. It's important that you tell the people you live with that you are starting a new routine and ask for their help in sticking to it. If you were on a diet, they would understand why you weren't eating dessert, and now you need to make them understand that there are certain things you will no longer be doing.

Leisure time

What are you spending your leisure time doing that really, if you're honest with yourself, is probably a waste of time? If you're a football fan, do you (a) watch a match on TV every now and then, (b) watch your team every week, (c) read the sports pages every day and watch every match that's on telly, or (d) all of the above, plus a daily flutter as well as scouring the internet for the latest team news? Clearly, there are different levels at which you can enjoy your leisure time, and – equally clearly – it seems to me that some people's leisure consumption could be drastically reduced. Just as too much chocolate cake is a bad thing if you want to lose weight, too much time spent on frivolous things is a bad thing if you want to save time.

■ Men are in paid employment for 1 hour and 17 minutes longer per day than women in Britain, while women spend over an hour and half longer than men on housework. *The UK Time Use Survey, 2000*

Now is the time to cancel magazine subscriptions and resign your membership of clubs and organisations that are distracting you from the things you have identified that really matter to you. If you are aware that you are watching a lot of television, ask yourself why. Is it habit? Is it because you really enjoy it? Ask yourself if you really, really care about the characters in *EastEnders* or if someone wins a big prize on *Deal Or No Deal*, or do you care more about making a difference in your own life?

Just as with food diets, there are things you can do to make it harder for you to fall back into old habits. If you don't buy biscuits, then they're not in the house so you can't eat them. Can you do something about your leisure habits that make them harder to indulge in? If you are a TV addict, perhaps you should consider giving your TV away, which is what I did when I was starting my first business. I sold it to raise some cash, but I soon realised the benefit wasn't financial. I had so much more time to devote to my business and when I got home at night I renovated the house instead of vegging out, and those renovations made me even more money. Even if it's only temporary, living without a TV for a while would really show you how much time you could free up. If that's too drastic, how about giving away your set-top box and seeing how you get on with just the terrestrial channels for a while. Or moving the TV into a room where it's uncomfortable to sit down for too long. Of course, if you have subscription TV, cancelling your subscription would save you time *and* money.

Can you find a way to cut out TV the way you might cut out puddings? If that seems impossible, could you significantly cut down your TV habit and maybe only have a pudding once or twice a week?

Work

The workplace is full of distractions that can waste your – and your company's – time. There's gossip for starters, then there are tedious meetings that achieve nothing, reports to read that don't come to any conclusions and dealing with clients who don't produce much revenue.

When most people complain about work, it's usually because something is stopping them working. Whether it's a scheming co-worker or an inefficient boss, what we hate about work is rarely having too much of it, it's usually about *not* being able to do enough of it. So let's look at what's slowing you down at work.

Colleagues

They may be your friends, but are you too easily distracted by them, or persuaded by them to do things you shouldn't? If so, how can you reduce your colleague calories? Could you work somewhere else, possibly nearer the boss, to avoid interference? Could you start bringing in a packed lunch so you don't spend so long in the canteen? Could you plug yourself into an MP3 player to shut out their chatter? Or explain, politely, that you want to work instead of talk? Work out a way of putting the distraction out of reach, doing the equivalent of putting the biscuit tin in the shed so you won't be tempted.

Clients

Have you heard of the 80/20 principle that says 80% of your income comes from 20% of your clients? It doesn't always hold true, but it is often the case that some of your clients will be a lot more valuable to you than others. If that's true for you, you know who you should be spending your time on. It may even be that some of your clients are wasting your time and that you should actually let that part of your business go so you can concentrate on clients who bring you a greater income, greater kudos or greater exposure. Ask yourself who is more bother than they're worth.

Your employer

Some companies have very strange, and very inefficient, management structures. If you find yourself reporting to two different managers, or being asked to do work that you weren't trained to do, the chances are that your employer is wasting your time. You have three choices in this sort of situation: work around it, work to change it or work somewhere else.

If you can suggest ways in which systems and procedures can be improved, you may impress your employer and get a bonus or a promotion – but there's also a chance you'll be seen as a troublemaker. If you are not appreciated, you should probably look around for a job where you will be. In the meantime, ask yourself what you can do to make the situation work for you. Instead of spending your time complaining, spend time finding solutions that let you get more out of your job.

Friends

Our friends aren't always good company. Peer pressure has been shown in numerous studies as a major reason why we do the things we do: either because we want to impress someone or because we want to be in with the 'in crowd' or because we just don't want to be left behind. It's no wonder, then, that many people are led away from their goals by their mates.

Some people have what I can only call toxic friends. At some point in our lives we've probably all been egged on by a charismatic friend to do something we regret, whether it's staying for another drink or buying something we really couldn't afford. If you have toxic friends, you need to devise ways to resist the easy temptation to go out and have a good time.

Sticking to your diet

Diets always sound good on paper, but every now and then you find yourself bumping into a chocolate cake or a bag of chips, and you just can't help yourself. And once you've eaten one cake, the diet's been ruined so you may as well eat another! It's the same with a time diet and you need to know what to do when a friend asks you for a beer that takes you away from your goals, or a client calls and demands attention you don't have time to give.

You need to resist short-term pleasures so that you can reap the long-term benefits, just as a dieter chooses between the immediate pleasure of a bag of chips and the long-term pleasure of losing weight; you have to look to the future for the strength to resist distractions. The way to do this is to focus on your goals. Remind yourself what you want to achieve, the kind of life you will be able to create if you stick to your guns and don't waste your time on things that don't matter. Think about those mental photos I urged you to create in the first chapter. Keep in mind the life you have imagined for yourself and it will be easier to say no to those calorific distractions.

CHECKLIST

✔ A time detox is like a diet detox – you cut out the activities that are bad for you

✔ Taking each area of your life in turn, identify the activities that are taking up too much of your time unnecessarily

✔ Focusing on your goals and long-term gains can motivate you to resist short-term temptations

PART TWO

What are you doing today?

1
What did you do yesterday?

The first half of this book was about finding ways and developing techniques to ensure that you get what you want out of life. From now on, I want to concentrate on the skills and attitudes that will help you make the most of every day. This is where the parallels between a food diet and a time diet are going to become obvious: from now on it's all about finding a template that works for you. And just as many food diets encourage you keep track of everything you eat, I want you to start this new section by keeping a record of everything you do: before we can make tomorrow more productive than today, we need to understand where we went wrong yesterday.

Start by jotting down a list of everything you did yesterday. Absolutely everything: even include everyday things like washing and brushing your teeth. Then write down an estimate of how long each task took. Start from the moment you woke up to the moment you went to bed. Now add up the time spent on tasks.

■ Women spend more time washing and dressing than men. The difference in time spent on these activities is more pronounced in teenagers, when the average 19-year-old woman spends 40 minutes more a day on washing and dressing than the average 19-year-old man. The average difference between the genders across all age ranges is 10 minutes a day. *The UK Time Use Survey, 2000*

Calculate how long you were asleep and deduct this amount from your total of twenty-four hours, then deduct the total time spent on tasks. How much time have you got left? In theory you shouldn't have any time left, but I asked five people to do this simple exercise for me and the missing hours in their lives ranged from two hours to four hours and fifteen minutes! The fact is that we spend so much of our time on mundane or pointless tasks and activities that we can't even remember doing them! So the only way really to work out how you are spending your time is consciously to measure it. And the way to do that is to keep a time diary.

EXERCISE 6 – Keeping a time diary

I warn you now: this is a bit of an undertaking, but, as with all things that require a bit of effort, the results are significant. Over the next week, I want you to choose three days on which you are going to itemise every single thing you do. From the time you get up to the time you go to bed, you are going to account for every minute.

The problem with keeping such a detailed diary is that you find yourself going 'Blimey! It's four o'clock and I haven't made a note since midday! What have I been up to?' I've been keeping a diary myself, and these are my suggestions for making sure you keep updating your diary throughout the day.

- Every time you look at a clock, use it as a trigger to make an entry
- Set an alarm to go off on your mobile phone every hour (or use a kitchen timer) and immediately write down everything you've done since your last entry
- I found it helped to make a note every time I returned to my desk. I had a document open on my computer and just added to it every time I sat down

You might find it's convenient to get a pocket-sized notebook that you can keep with you throughout the day. If you can do this for three days out of the next seven (making sure at least one of them is a day when you are at work), you can start to see how you really spend your time. This works best if you don't just put in entries like 'reading report' but are specific with entries like 'read three pages of report'. By including this kind of detail you might be able to identify patterns and notice that you get much more reading done after lunch, or when you are on your own, or while you are on a train. I asked a few guinea pigs to do this for me and what follows is a page from a diary from an employee who had to write a report for me on this particular day.

07.00	*Alarm*
07.10	*Get up. Shower*
07.40	*Breakfast, listen to radio, read the paper*
08.25	*Walk to work*
08.50	*Get to desk. Sort out paperwork*
09.00	*Check emails*
09.15	*Surf*
09.50	*Do research for report*
10.00	*Look at BBC news online*
10.35	*Chat to colleagues*
11.00	*Look at CNN online*
11.05	*Make a cup of tea*
11.15	*Think*
11.30	*Write 158 words of report*
11.35	*Phone call*
11.50	*Word total now 343*
12.55	*Lunch*
13.15	*556 words*
13.28	*581 words*
13.42	*900 words*

14.05	*1162 words*
14.15	*Daydream*
15.00	*1512 words*
15.15	*Cup of tea, chat*
15.27	*1705 words*
15.45	*1884 words*
15.55	*Daydream*
16.05	*2009 words*
16.15	*Chat with colleagues*
16.20	*2036 words. Leave office*
17.40	*Physiotherapy appointment*
18.20	*Walk home*
18.40	*Watch the news*
19.21	*Surf/Facebook*
20.05	*Tidy up, clean the bathroom*
21.05	*Dinner and wash up*
22.00	*Watch TV*
23.00	*Start getting ready for bed. Read. Sleep.*

I wish I could get all my employees to do this, because it's clear this woman works incredibly well after lunch. I asked her about this and she reckons it's because the first few hours of the day are often unsettled with other people arriving and talking about the night before, which is why she tries to get into the office early to get her paperwork done before the rest of her team arrive.

What alarmed her – and me! – is that she was in the office for 7.5 hours, from 8.50 a.m. to 4.20 p.m. but she only spent three hours and twenty-six minutes writing the report. Over half her day was spent chatting, daydreaming and eating and drinking. If she could find a way of structuring her day better, she could get a lot more done, impress her boss and land herself a promotion or a pay rise. Or maybe she could persuade her boss (not likely in this case!) that she could go part-time and still get the same amount of work done.

The important thing to remember here is that she did get the report done on the day she said she would, but I would love to see her work to her full potential; and the great thing is that, since she started keeping this diary, she has really upped her work rate just because she is now aware of the time she had been wasting. Four hours frittered away each day adds up to twenty hours every working week – which adds up to a frightening forty full days a year or a shocking 120 working days a year!

The more days you keep a time diary for, the more useful it becomes. Perhaps you will notice that you get more done in the afternoon, or that you are productive when you work alone, or that you spend too long shopping, or cooking, or watching TV. If you notice that there are particular times of the day when you consistently waste time, perhaps you should consider rearranging your day. If, for example, the hours after 10.00 p.m. are spent in front of the TV watching nothing very much until you are tired enough to go to bed, perhaps you should consider going to bed at 10.00 p.m. and getting up at 6.00 a.m. You might find the hours between 6.00 and 8.00 a.m. can be more productive than the time after 10.00 p.m.

It's not always possible to play around with your daily routine as you'll probably have to fit in with other members of your family, but if you can be flexible why not try changing the hours you keep? Over the years I've heard stories from people whose hours were changed for them – often by having kids or working shifts – who found that keeping unusual hours made them more productive. In large parts of the Mediterranean, the siesta is an integral part of the working day and many people find that splitting their working day into two parts with a long break in between boosts their energy levels, meaning they get more done in the afternoon. If you can, play around with your schedule – you may just find a new way of working that helps you get more done, effortlessly.

CHECKLIST

✔ We do so many things without thinking that they can be difficult to recall accurately

✔ The only way really to see where the time goes is to keep a time diary

✔ A time diary lets you spot patterns in your time use that will enable you to plan activities more efficiently

✔ Changing your daily routine could free up several hours each day

2
Scheduling and planning

Now **that you've identified** the ways in which you squandered time yesterday, it's important to learn the rules and tools that will help you ensure you don't make the same mistakes tomorrow. The next three chapters will take you through the time-management techniques that will make you more efficient. Taken together, these chapters will give you a complete set of skills that might just change your life.

I want to start by tackling your planning and scheduling skills. Do you plan your working day? If you don't, the chances are that you waste a lot of time. Planning your work involves taking your diary (i.e. your scheduled appointments), and your 'to do' list (your unscheduled work) and working out what you're going to do when. If, for example, your diary tells you that a major client is going on holiday for two weeks and you know that means a fortnight of far fewer interruptions, then that's an opportunity to concentrate on work that needs peace and quiet, or it's a chance to clear your backlog. Just a few minutes' planning ahead with your diary can help you prioritise and schedule work more efficiently.

Good scheduling, on the other hand, involves setting aside times in your day to deal with email, to make phone calls, to reduce your backlog etc. The more you can schedule your work into specific zones, the more efficient you will become. Once you've identified these zones, give a few moments' thought as to the best sequence for these tasks so that you carry them out in a logical order. And all you need is a diary, a pencil and a rubber; a BlackBerry or iPhone work just as well.

Scheduling

If you buy yourself a decent-sized diary that shows a day on a single page (or use an electronic equivalent), you will have enough room to write down every commitment you've made. Then, whenever you are asked to do something new, you just look at your diary and see if you have enough unallocated time to do it. In a nutshell, that's all there is to it, but by putting a bit more effort into your planning and scheduling you can turn your diary into a much more valuable time-management tool. These are the things you should be looking out for as you fill up your diary:

1 Use a pencil

When using a paper diary, the key thing is to use a pencil and not a pen (obviously with an electronic diary you can move appointments round endlessly) as you want to be able to rearrange events easily. When you get new invitations, or find out more information about the events you will be attending, you may need to reschedule.

■ The average UK worker does 3 hours and 15 minutes unpaid over-time each week. That adds up to one month's work – for free – a year!

2009 Survey for Teletext Holidays

2 Timing

When most people put something in their diary, they will write '4.00 p.m. Hair appointment'. When I write something in my diary, I don't just write down when something starts, I write down when it ends. When I am asked to attend a function, I always ask how long they will need me for. This has two advantages: it makes them think carefully about how they want to use my time and means I get more out of the event, but it also means I know I can safely schedule in another appointment afterwards. If I'm asked to attend a function at a venue I don't know, the first thing I do is find out how long it will take me to get there. It's the only way to make sure that a thirty-minute meeting doesn't end up taking up half the day.

3 Immovables

Most things in life are surprisingly negotiable, but we all have a few commitments that cannot be shifted. We can't change the dates of the school term, for instance, or things we've been invited to, like weddings or birthday parties. While these events aren't flexible, they can be very useful when it comes to planning. I use these immovable events as hooks on which to hang the rest of my commitments. For instance, if I know I'm going to be in London filming *Dragons' Den*, this gives me a reason to schedule other things I need to do in London around my filming commitments. If my agent, who is based in London, wants to take me to lunch, I'm not going to travel to London just for lunch – I will fit him in when I'm already there for something else.

4 Clusters

Wherever possible, I plan to do similar activities in clusters. As you'll see in the next chapter, I use my diary in conjunction with my 'to do' list and whenever I have to find time for a new event or activity, I look in my diary for a similar event or activity. If I'm already going to be wearing a suit for one meeting, it makes sense to schedule another meeting I need to be wearing a suit for right afterwards rather than something I'd wear casual clothes to. If there are lots of smaller tasks that all need to be done in the office, then I look for a couple of hours when I don't have meetings and cluster all the little tasks together.

Just as computers are more efficient when their hard drives are defragmented, so are human beings. Research has shown that when we try and do too many things at once, our brains don't cope as well. 'Multi-tasking' – such as thinking about a loan application in between interviewing job candidates and replying to emails – can see our IQs drop by as much as ten points, and that means we aren't making the smartest decisions or applying ourselves as well as we might if we just focused on one thing at a time. The ability to focus – one of the elements of smart time-keeping – is critical to making progress, which is why I think clustering similar tasks together allows us to be more efficient.

Planning

It's all very well loading your diary with appointments, but to be really time-efficient you need to plan as well as schedule, and planning is all about anticipation. If you were starting a new diet, you would probably sit down with your new diet recipe book and plan your meals for the week; you need to do something similar with your time diet.

Planning is about stocking the fridge to make sure you've got all the ingredients you need for your week to run to schedule. For instance, as filming on *Dragons' Den* frequently overruns, I have learnt that I often don't have time to go home and change before going out in the evening. The solution? Good planning now means that I keep a change of clothes and a bag of toiletries at the studio so that I can go out straight after work. Everyone could keep some toiletries at work so that they can save an unnecessary trip home.

You should look for patterns in your workload to see if you can be more efficient. For example, if you are going to London for a meeting, can you rearrange other meetings to take place on the same day rather than making several trips? Are there certain jobs that require the same tools? If so, it makes sense to do them at the same time. What you want to try to do is defragment your time so that similar tasks are carried out in blocks rather than in a piecemeal fashion. You should try and identify:

- Tasks that take place at the same location
- Tasks that can be done wearing the same clothing
- Tasks that need cooperation from the same person
- Tasks that need peace and quiet
- Computer-/desk-/phone-based tasks

Planning is also about anticipation and making sure you have enough time to do the things you want to do. As a quick exercise, take a look at the activities in your diary for tomorrow and estimate how long each of those tasks will take. Then just ask yourself a simple question: do I have enough time? By doing this every morning (or, ideally, further in advance than that), you can anticipate if you're going to have trouble making your deadlines. If you are, you can make contingencies. The first thing to do is identify tasks you can delegate, and then any that can be rescheduled. After all, isn't it much nicer when a friend cancels a date in the morning rather than when you're sitting at a table in a restaurant waiting for him? And if you know a colleague is waiting for you to complete a piece of work before she can start on something, any advance warning you can give really helps her out. But it also helps you out, too: by communicating your delay, you take some of the pressure off yourself which means you'll be less flustered and more able to focus.

There is another question you should ask yourself as you add entries to your diary: what's going to stop you? The phone rings, the kids get sick, the boiler packs up: often it seems that whenever we've made plans of our own, life has made other plans for us.

If you can anticipate the distractions, you can (a) make sure you avoid them, or (b) know how you will respond to problems when they crop up. This is far more efficient than getting into a flap and reduces the chances that you'll make a poor decision under pressure.

My diary

Because I write down how long everything takes in my diary, the days when I'm filming don't just say 'Filming at Pinewood'. Instead my diary says: 'Car at 7.30 a.m., Hair & makeup, 8.30, Filming 9 to 12, Lunch 12 to 1.45, Filming 1.45 until the end of the day'. When I see a long lunch in my schedule, I arrange for my personal trainer to come to the studio and I do a workout instead of hanging around waiting for filming to begin. I know most people don't have a personal trainer, but we could all go for a walk or a run in our lunch hour.

The more you can anticipate how your day will pan out, the more you will fit into it. I've already said that I hate wasting time and that's why I think it pays to plan ahead. I've even got to the stage where I hate waiting for lifts, so much so, in fact, that I press the call button on the lift at my London flat before I check the post box. By the time I've collected my letters, the lift has arrived. It might only save thirty seconds, but when you hate wasting time as much as I do, that matters!

To show you just how important I think planning is, I want to take you through a week from my diary to show just how much more you can fit in if you take a few minutes to plan ahead.

Monday 15 June 2009

9.45 a.m.	*Car to collect from hotel to drive to location*
9.45–10.30	*Paperwork/returning calls while in the car*
10.30–1.30 p.m.	DD *filming in Nottingham with Magnamole. Wear* DD *suit and tie*
1.30	*Car to take me to office*
1.30–1.45	*Phone call with land broker*
1.45–2.15	*Read report from Tony Earnshaw, MD of my investment in UK Commercial Cleaning Services*
2.15–2.35	*Phone call with my PA Kim*
2.35–3.00	*Conference call with hotel team*
3.00–3.20	*Return calls/emails*
3.20	*Arrive office*
3.30–3.50	*Meeting with PD*
3.50–4.10	*Meeting with FD*
4.10–4.30	*Catch-up meeting with MD*
4.30–5.00	*Paperwork/diary planning with Kim*
5.00–5.30	*Follow-up on Magnamole calls*

The first thing to say here is that, whenever I can, I always use a driver. Obviously this is a luxury most people can't afford, but for me it is worth the expense because I can use the time in the car to work. On this occasion I called my PA Kim at 9.30 a.m. before the car arrived to go through the morning post.

Once in the back of the car, I worked on my BlackBerry replying to emails because I knew that as soon as I started filming I would have to turn it off. During filming there are always breaks for technical reasons, and these breaks are a good opportunity to talk to the management team at Magnamole, one of my investments from the show, and help them with their business strategy. I promised to make some calls on their behalf that I scheduled in for the end of the day. The driver took me straight to my office in Darlington while I had a scheduled phone call with a land broker. The rest of the time in the car was spent reading and checking in with my PA. Once at the office, I grabbed a sandwich from the Bannatyne Health Club which is right next door to my office and took it to my desk as I had back-to-back meetings – all twenty minutes long as I have worked out this is an optimum length for a meeting (see p. 143) – with my Projects Director, Finance Director and MD. At 5.00 p.m. I put in the Magnamole calls I had promised to make. I always have my workout clothes at the office, and at 5.30 I went for a workout. I was home by 7.00 p.m. and spent an hour and a half with the kids before they went to bed. I watched a bit of TV that evening, but instead of watching whatever was on, my wife and I watched a programme we'd recorded on Sky+. I never watch live TV any more – technology means that TV fits into my schedule and never the other way round.

Tuesday 16 June 2009

9.30–10.00 a.m.	*Paperwork and letters with Kim*
10.00–10.20	*Meeting with entrepreneurs seeking finance*
10.20–10.40	*Phone call with charity manager*
10.40–11.00	*Catch-up meeting with MD, FD, PD*
11.00–11.30	*Interview via office landline with* Edinburgh Evening News *about the Edinburgh spa*

11.30–12.00 p.m.	*Interview with* Edinburgh Magazine *for their Treasure Trove section, to mention the spa*
12.00–12.45	*Sign letters. Phone calls and emails*
1.02	*Train from Darlington to Edinburgh Waverley Station*
3.10	*Arrive Edinburgh. Staying at Balmoral Hotel*
6.00–9.00	*Launch of Edinburgh Queen Street Spa*

Whenever I see a late start in my diary I know it means I can get the kids ready and take them to school. Not only do I get to spend time with them (which was important on that occasion as we were about to spend a couple of nights away from them while their grandparents looked after them), but their school is on their way to my office, so it saves a trip – and that saves time. I spent the first half-hour in the office with Kim going through the post and dictating letters before a scheduled meeting with two entrepreneurs who had approached me for finance. I was very glad of my twenty-minute meeting limit, as it was pretty clear, pretty quickly, that I wouldn't invest. I then took a scheduled call from a manager at one of the charities I work with to discuss my involvement in a new fundraising campaign. I then had a quick meeting with my senior managers to update each other on our activities. I then did a couple of media interviews over the phone. Wherever possible, I schedule media interviews back-to-back as this has two advantages: (1) they can take place in the same location, especially when they're done over the phone; and (2) I can tell the journalist that I have to end the interview because the next one is waiting! I had just under an hour before I had to leave for the station, which is five minutes from my office, and that was enough time to sign paperwork and make some phone calls. On the train, I caught up with reading and talked to my wife who was travelling with me. We chose to stay at the Balmoral Hotel because it is right next to Waverley Station, which meant that, within five minutes of getting off the train, I was in my hotel room. After a quick freshen-up I was out on the pavement walking to one of my clubs to take a look around and catch up with the staff. Whenever I have spare time and I'm in the vicinity of one of my health clubs, I always use it as an opportunity to see how the staff and members are getting on. After that it was back to the hotel to get ready for the launch party of our new spa in Edinburgh. A party like that is always a chance to do a bit of work – speaking to journalists, meeting new members of staff and potential customers. As I still hadn't eaten, I invited the new spa manager to have dinner with me, my MD and some of our suppliers – that's the kind of multi-tasking I can cope with!

Wednesday 17 June 2009

9.00 a.m.	*Train to Glasgow*
10.00–5.00 p.m.	*Glasgow taxi outing annual fundraising event.*
	Meet at Kelvin Way
6.50–8.10	*Check-in opens*
8.50 Depart	*Glasgow Airport on BA flight*
10.10 Arrive	*London Heathrow*

This is an example of an 'immovable' fixture in my diary. This was a fantastic day when taxi drivers from all over Glasgow (a job I used to do) took kids from disadvantaged backgrounds out for the day. I knew it was something I wanted to be a part of so I had agreed to do it a year before. It was because this was already in my diary that I scheduled the spa launch in Edinburgh the day before. We could have had the launch any day that month, but it made sense to do it when I was already going to be in Scotland for the taxi outing. After breakfast we took the train through to Glasgow and I used the journey to check in with my PA and go through urgent correspondence and dictate letters. We could have got a driver to take us, but as we were right next to the station (and city-centre driving is always a pain) the train was quicker. A cab at the other end took us to our destination. It was a day when I didn't want to be interrupted by the office unless it was an emergency, so that I could give my attention to the charity and enjoy being with the kids. I ordered a cab to get me to the airport just as check-in was closing. I never get to the airport when check-in opens as you only have to queue! The plane was slightly delayed and we didn't get into Heathrow until after 11.00 p.m. and took a taxi to my London flat.

Thursday 18 June 2009

9.30–10.00 a.m.	*Phone call with Kim*
10.30–11.30	*Car to Ascot (Ladies Day). Phone calls*
2.30 p.m.	*First race*
5.30	*Last race. Driver will wait to collect and take to the flat in London*
7.00	*Terrence Higgins Trust Friends for Life dinner, Grosvenor House Hotel. Dress code: lounge suit. Driver will take, wait and return to flat*

The reason we'd flown to London the night before was because we had invitations for Ladies Day at Ascot, something we were both excited about doing. But as my priority that day was to attend the THT event (I am a patron of the charity), I knew I would need a driver if we were going to fit both events in. Thankfully my wife got up early in the morning as she had a hair appointment. I say thankfully because it meant I had time to realise that I didn't have a dress suit in London – but I still had time to buy one! My diary had only specified the dress code for the evening event, not the day one – so that cost me time and money! Always write everything pertinent in your diary! As our flat is in central London, I didn't have to walk far before I found an outfitter, but it did mean my phone call to Kim took place while I was on the go. The car arrived at 10.30 a.m. to take us to Ascot and I had calls booked in for the journey with my agent, an after-dinner speaking agency and the producer of a TV show I was making.

■ 21% of Americans have missed vital work deadlines because they were disorganised. Of those people, nearly half said that disorganisation causes them to work late at least twice a week.

2006 Esselte Survey

Friday 19 June 2009

10.00–10.30 a.m.	*Phone call with Kim*
10.30–11.30	*Meeting at flat with Grant Morgan*
11.30–12.15 p.m.	*Emails, paperwork, returning calls*
12.15	*Car will collect from the flat*
12.20–1.00	*Phone call with DD investors*
1.00–3.00	*Filming at Toni & Guy, 28 Kensington Church Street, London W8 (for Tangle Teezers). Car to next location*
3.30–6.00	*Filming with Autosafe at Arlington Crescent, London NW9. Car booked to return to flat*
8.30	*Table booked at the Hospital Club, 24 Endell Street, London WC2*

The late start meant I could take my wife out for breakfast before taking her to the station to get the train back to Darlington and the kids. I then checked in with Kim before my meeting with Grant. Grant – who runs a watch company that I have a stake in – had so much to update me on that we scheduled a longer meeting, but I still had forty-five minutes to go through my backlog of calls and emails before I left the flat. In the car, I had two catch-up phone calls with entrepreneurs I have backed on *Dragons' Den*. The rest of the day was taken up filming a *Dragons' Den* update show, and, as well as making a TV programme, I also got to catch up with the entrepreneurs I backed on the show. Back at the flat, I had time to talk to my kids on the phone before going out. I had dinner with a potential business partner that night, and deliberately booked a restaurant within walking distance of my flat. In cities, so often the quickest way to get around is on foot – no traffic jams, no engineering works, no waiting around. If there is the option of walking to an appointment, I take it.

Saturday 20 June 2009

This was a very rare day for me, a day when there was absolutely nothing in my diary – no work, no social event. If I had been at home in Darlington that Saturday, I would have spent the day with my wife and kids, but I needed to stay in London for more filming on the Sunday. So after breakfast I took a walk to one of my central London clubs to check in with the staff and members. I had already downloaded the staff roster from our intranet, so I knew in advance who would – or at least should – be at work. I love dropping into my clubs unannounced to see how things are. I get weekly written reports from the managers, but there's nothing like an impromptu visit to see how things really are. After sorting out a few small problems and talking to members, I did a workout and then walked back to my flat. I passed a barber's, so popped in to get my hair cut and then bought the weekend papers. I read the papers while catching up on TV programmes I'd recorded. I ordered a takeaway and then got out my 'to do' list that reminded me I wanted to look at the bookings at the hotels I own. So I turned my computer on and found the data on our intranet. By analysing the booking patterns, occupancy rates and discount promotions, I was able to spot patterns that I knew would boost bookings in the future. After talking to the kids and watching a bit more TV, I had a very rare early night.

Sunday 21 June 2009

8.00 a.m.	*Car to take me to Ramsgate, Kent, for filming*
9.00–9.45	*Drop in on Broadstairs club*
10.00–6.00 p.m.	*Filming*
6.00	*Return to Broadstairs club*
8.00	*Car to London*
9.30	*Arrive at flat*

When I saw the location for filming a new series called *Save Our Seaside Resorts* I realised that it wasn't very far away from one of my clubs. So I called the chauffeur service and asked them to pick me up half an hour earlier so that I could stop off at my club in Broadstairs and see how things were going – after all, it saves a separate trip, and that saves time. I read the Sunday papers in the car and arrived in Broadstairs for break- fast and a time for a quick chat with the duty manager before I had to leave for filming. My phone is always switched off when I'm filming so any breaks between takes were used to talk to business owners in Ramsgate about the problems they were facing. The premise of *SOSR* is that my business expertise can help attract more holidaymakers to the area and so every spare minute was spent talking to people and finding ways to solve their problems. At the end of an eight-hour shoot I was exhausted, and I knew just the place to relax: it was back to the club in Broadstairs where there is an outdoor heated swimming pool. I had dinner at the club before being driven back to London.

If you're wondering why I spend my spare time checking hotel occupancy rates and dropping in on my clubs, it's because – after providing for my family and spending time with them

– my goal is to grow my businesses and to be the best entrepreneur I can be. By dedicating myself to my businesses I get to see what works at one club so that it can be replicated at the rest, and I get to see what doesn't work and what other managers need to be aware of. And by growing the businesses I have more money to spend on the charity projects that are close to my heart. My goals inspire me to achieve more, which is why I have learnt to plan ahead.

 CHECKLIST

✔ **Be specific when you write things in your diary. Always estimate how long an activity will last**

✔ **Schedule similar activities together**

✔ **Anticipate what you will need for each event in your diary as this will save you time**

3
The turbo-powered 'to do' list

am a big fan of making a 'to do' list. Whenever anyone asks
me to do something, or it occurs to me that something
needs to be done, I make a note of it. I usually have an A4
notebook with me, but if I'm on the run I make a note on my
BlackBerry or occasionally phone myself and leave a message
so that when I get home, or back to my desk, I can add the note
to my list.

I rely on making lists to make sure I don't forget about anything, but there's no point having a 'to do' list if you don't have
a strategy for making sure the things on your list actually get
done. I know there are some people who think 'to do' lists are
unhelpful as, inevitably, there are tasks left undone which ultimately accumulate into an unmanageable backlog . . . which is
why the chapter that follows is about clearing your backlog *and*
making sure another backlog doesn't mount up.

■ A global survey showed that most people use 60% – or less – of
their available work time. More than 38,000 people in 200 countries
said that even though they were in the office 5 days a week, they
were only productive for 3 of them. *Microsoft Survey, 2005*

On its own, the 'to do' list can only help you so much; for
me it really only becomes a tool for getting things done when
I use it in conjunction with my diary. Your diary contains your
scheduled work and your 'to do' list your *unscheduled* work. As

the best way I know of making sure things get done is to allocate a time to do them, the more tasks you can move to your diary, the more likely it is that you will get them done. If at the end of the day you did not do something in your diary, you move it to your 'to do' list to be rescheduled. And if you look at your diary and see some unscheduled time, that's the moment you get out your 'to do' list and start ticking tasks off.

The longest 'to do' list in the world

I want you to start by making a list of everything you've been meaning to do for the past few months. In no particular order, write down everything, from tidying your desk to asking for a pay rise to changing your car insurance. Whether it's a big job (such as decorating the outside of your house) or a small job (such as getting a quote for someone else to decorate the outside of your house), you need to write down all your outstanding tasks. The more complete your list, the more helpful the next few paragraphs will be. I asked my friend Joe (who will readily admit he's not the most efficient guy in the world) to do this exercise, and this is his 'to do' list.

EXAMPLE 1 – 'to do' list

Check domain name availability
Get quotes from web developers
Phone round estate agents
Get confirmation of holiday
Get eye test
Get quote for garden work
Sort out shed
Buy suit for Billy's wedding
Speak to Mum about house-sitting

Book kennels
Get tickets for theatre
Tax return
Transfer bank accounts
Buy Suzi's birthday present
Print out photos
Read financial report from Daniel
Get someone to fix the bathroom door
Parents' evening at Jess's school
Tidy desk
Sort out/clear out filing cabinet
Tess and David over for dinner
Find hotel for anniversary
Join football team/get fit
Quiz night at the pub
Set up the Wii
Buy HDD recorder
Get car serviced
Read the book Jackie gave me for Christmas

And this shows brilliantly how a basic 'to do' list can be almost useless. Where on earth do you start? This is more of an 'undone' list! If your 'to do' list looks like this, here are some quick steps to make it look a bit more manageable – and a lot more useful.

STEP 1

When you look at your list, can you see any pattern to the tasks you have left undone? For instance:

(a) Are you good at sorting things out at work but rubbish at home?

(b) Have you been ignoring tasks that involve asking for help?

(c) Are the things you have neglected perhaps all dependent on spending money?

In many cases there are obvious reasons why we are letting areas of our life slide while coping very well in other areas. Keep looking until you can spot a pattern. For a lot of people, dealing with their time-keeping issues means identifying and treating the underlying cause of their time-keeping issues. If we take the examples above, the solutions to these time-wasting issues could be:

(a) You need to have the same kind of structure and oversight at home that motivates you at work

(b) You need to overcome your shyness or politeness or ego, and find ways that enable you to ask for help when you need it

(c) You need to get your finances sorted before you can do the things you want to get done

In Joe's case, he's got a lot of tasks that could be dealt with, or scheduled, if he made a few phone calls. If he could schedule fifteen minutes a day for making phone calls, he'd start to perform better. If you can spot an obvious pattern on your 'undone' list, and then work out the cause behind that pattern and address it, you can start to make big changes very quickly.

STEP 2

The next step is to try and reduce the number of items on your list, and the quickest way to do that is to delegate them to someone else. Whether they're tasks that need to be accomplished at work or at home, ask yourself if there is anyone in your life who is better suited to carrying out certain tasks. Just make sure that when you hand over responsibility for these tasks the person you are handing them over to knows what is expected from him or her – and when. Turn to Chapter 10, on Delegation (p. 51) to remind yourself of the best way to go about doing this.

These were the tasks on Joe's list that he delegated to colleagues and members of his family:

EXAMPLE 2 – **tasks to delegate**

Get confirmation of holiday
Get quote for garden work
Book kennels
Get tickets for theatre
Get car serviced
Print out photos
Set up the Wii

Now let's see how many other tasks we can remove. Looking closely at your list, how many of the outstanding tasks are you very unlikely to get round to in the near future? Often the jobs that get left on our 'to do' lists are low-priority, non-time-specific tasks that would be more appropriate on a wish list rather than a 'to do' list. So create a wish list and move all those 'wouldn't it be nice if they were done' jobs on to your wish list because, if you're really not going to get round to doing them, then all they're doing is clogging up your 'to do' list and making it harder for you to see what really needs to be done.

■ Office distractions take up 2.1 hours of the average American's working day. The cost of those interruptions to the US economy has been estimated at $588 billion a year. *Basex Research, 2005*

These are the tasks Joe moved to his wish list:

EXAMPLE 3 – wish list

Sort out shed
Transfer bank accounts
Get someone to fix the bathroom door
Join football team/get fit
Buy HDD recorder
Read the book Jackie gave me for Christmas

If you put your wish list somewhere safe, you will never be short of something to do: as soon as you find yourself with a spare afternoon or some annual leave to use up, then you can start attending to these tasks. In the meantime, you've got something more important to get on with: step 3.

STEP 3

Hopefully, by now you have reduced the number of tasks on your 'to do' list quite considerably and you are already feeling more positive about your chances of getting everything done. The next step is to move more items from your list to your diary. It might take a few phone calls (to book an eye test in this example) but, by agreeing or finding out dates, you can whittle down your list further. Here are the tasks from Joe's list that can fairly quickly be transferred to the diary:

Get eye test
Parents' evening at Jess's school
Tess and David over for dinner
Quiz night at the pub

The more you can turn your unscheduled tasks into scheduled tasks, the more it becomes likely that you will actually do them.

STEP 4

Estimate how long each of the tasks you have left on your list will take you to complete and add up the total. The figure is important because that's how much time you need to find with the time-saving techniques that make up the rest of this book.

These are the tasks left on Joe's 'to do' list:

EXAMPLE 4 – edited 'to do' list

Check domain name availability	2 mins
Get quotes from web developers	3–6 hours
Phone round estate agents	1–2 hours
Buy suit for Billy's wedding	2–3 hours
Speak to Mum about house-sitting	15 mins
Tax return	2–4 hours
Buy Suzi's birthday present	2 hours
Print out photos	2 hours
Read financial report from Daniel	1 hour
Tidy desk	30 mins
Sort out/clear out filing cabinet	2 hours
Find hotel for anniversary	30 mins
TOTAL	**20 hours and 17 minutes**

If my friend could find a little over twenty hours through the time-saving techniques that make up the rest of this book, his 'to do' list would be cleared and he would have more time to devote to pursuing his goals.

STEP 5

Now group the tasks according to how long they will take to complete. Make separate lists of five-minute tasks, one-hour tasks, half-day tasks, one-day tasks and tasks that will take longer than that to complete. If you find yourself with a spare five minutes, look at your five-minute list. An hour might be all you need to clear the entire list. Once you've estimated how long each task will take, it's easier to see how you can slot your backlog into your new routine. It might also help to group activities together according to where you need to do them, either at home, at work or somewhere else. The more you can group tasks together into blocks of tasks, the easier it is to complete them all without interruption. Within a few days there should only be one place to put your five-minute and one-hour lists – in the bin!

STEP 6

Once you've ticked off the quick tasks, it's time to prioritise the more demanding tasks. Most people usually have a sense of what their priorities are – as a general rule, things that take you towards your goals take precedence – but it's not always clear-cut. In the list Joe gave me, for example, I don't know how urgently he needs to buy a suit for the wedding because I don't know when the wedding is. If it's three months away, it's not an urgent task; if it's this weekend then it goes right to the top of the list.

The way to prioritise is to weigh up the task's importance and its urgency. There are no hard and fast rules, but if you are having difficulty deciding what to concentrate on first, you could try this technique. Create two columns, one for importance and the other for urgency, and then give each task on your list a score in both columns out of a maximum of five.

	IMPORTANCE	URGENCY	TOTAL
Check domain name availability	3	3	6
Get quotes from web developers	4	3	7
Phone round estate agents	4	1	5
Buy suit for Billy's wedding	2	5	7
Speak to Mum about house-sitting	4	2	6
Tax return	5	3	8
Buy Suzi's birthday present	3	4	7
Print out photos	3	2	5
Read financial report from Daniel	5	4	9
Tidy desk	2	3	5
Sort out/clear out filing cabinet	3	2	5
Find hotel for anniversary	4	4	8

If you reorder the list according to each score, it's easy to see what needs to be done first:

Read financial report from Daniel	9
Tax return	8
Find hotel for anniversary	8
Get quotes from web developers	7
Buy suit for Billy's wedding	7
Buy Suzi's birthday present	7
Check domain name availability	6
Speak to Mum about house-sitting	6
Phone round estate agents	5
Print out photos	5
Tidy desk	5
Sort out/clear out filing cabinet	5

Now that you've got your 'to do' list into shape, you're ready to get it out whenever you have a gap in your diary. **Just a quick word of warning, though: if anything scores a five for** urgency, it doesn't matter what it scores for importance – you just have to do it right away.

You can add to your list throughout the day and, at the start of each new day, you can rewrite your list taking into account how your priorities have changed. Certain tasks will become more urgent with the passing of time (like buying a wedding outfit).

■ Employees spend an average of 11 minutes on a task before being distracted. Once distracted, it takes workers 25 minutes to return to the original task. *Research for the University of California*

By constantly moving your unscheduled work from your 'to do' list into your diary, you keep your list to a manageable size. If you ever find your list is getting out of hand, go through these steps and delegate where you can and move things to your wish list so that you can concentrate on the things that matter.

Once you've got your 'to do' list into shape, you are ready to take it up a gear. From now on, whenever you add a new task to your 'to do' list, you should include the date you added the task. If you don't include the date, it's entirely possible that less important tasks will keep being added to your 'to do' list but never get done. These low-priority tasks can clutter our minds as well as our lists, so you need a strategy for getting them ticked off. This is where the dates come in.

Nothing should stay on your list for more than a fortnight. If, when you make your new list each day, an item is fourteen days old you have a choice: either it's clear you are never going to get round to doing it and you have to tell anyone else involved that they need to get assistance from elsewhere; or you have to do it that very day. Look in your diary, find the gap and get it done. But if you don't get it done, let it go and don't let those little undone tasks clog up your life.

CHECKLIST

✔ When used with your diary, your 'to do' list becomes a powerful tool for getting things done

✔ Look for patterns in your 'undone' list to see if there are underlying reasons behind your poor use of time

✔ Reduce the size of your 'to do' list through delegation and the creation of a wish list

✔ Prioritise your tasks according to urgency and importance

✔ Once you're on top of your list, nothing should stay on it for more than a fortnight

4
Clearing your backlogs (and making sure they never come back)

The past two chapters have been about acquiring habits and techniques that will make you more efficient, but if you are still lugging your backlogs round with you, you're always going to be slowed down by them. Whatever your backlogs consist of – whether it's unanswered emails, your accounts or your laundry – clearing them is vital to freeing up your future to spend it on things that matter.

Backlogs mount up because we don't have the time to deal with things when they are presented to us. The moment you return from holiday to find hundreds of unread emails isn't likely to be the best time to try and read them all. And once a backlog has started, the chances of ever clearing it can seem hopeless and so you don't even bother to try, and emails build up to such a level that you almost can't bear to turn on your computer.

The nature of backlogs means they are unsorted: there's no way of telling which items in a random pile need your urgent attention, and which are just rubbish that can be deleted or ignored. This often means there's no obvious point of entry at which to start tackling your backlogs, and that means it's easier to let them carry on mounting up.

And yet sorting through backlogs is very straightforward. Here's how:

1 Draw a line

Whatever your backlog is made up of – bills, emails, invoices, laundry or unread books – you're never going to get through it if you keep adding to it with new items. So the first thing to do is to separate your backlog from new work. You draw a line between the old and the new so that you can start to deal with new work in an ordered way (see below). If email is your problem, then create a new folder and label it 'backlog'. If your in tray is overflowing, get a new in tray and label your old one 'backlog'. Once you have finished this book and freed up pockets of time throughout your day, you will be able to start allocating time to clearing your backlog.

2 Break the backlog down

The bigger the backlog, the more daunting it is to face. The way to get round this is not to say 'I'm going to clear my backlog today' as you probably won't believe yourself if you do. Instead, tell yourself that you're going to spend an hour on your backlog, or half an hour if that's all you can face. You might find that spending the first ten minutes of every day on the backlog whittles it down very quickly, or you might need to spend your lunchtime dealing with it. The important thing is that reducing your backlog should not interfere with you dealing efficiently with new work.

3 Start at the end

There's a tendency to think you should start clearing your backlog from the beginning, and, while this might seem logical to some, it doesn't make sense to me. If you've been ignoring something for several months, the chances are that you've either already missed the opportunity or it wasn't very important to start with. If someone really wanted your attention, they would have got back in touch. So it makes sense to start clearing the newest items on your backlog first as you are more likely to come across urgent or important tasks while there's still a chance to do something about them.

Clearing your backlog is such a great feeling. Not only is there an enormous sense of accomplishment, but it's also pretty liberating. You're no longer carrying around this drain on your resources, and you are no longer nagged by worries about what's actually in your backlog. And, of course, once it's cleared, you will have so much more time to spend on reaching your goals. You just need to make sure that another backlog doesn't build up . . .

■ Office workers switch activities, such as making a call, speaking with colleagues or working on a document, every 3 minutes on average. No wonder we find it hard to concentrate.

Research for the University of California

Preventing future backlogs from mounting up

There are three elements to preventing future backlogs from swallowing you up – planning, scheduling and developing better systems for incoming work. I've already talked a lot about planning and scheduling, so I won't say too much more about them here. The sorts of things you want to consider are planning ahead so that when, for example, you return from a holiday you schedule time to deal with the tasks that have mounted up in your absence. Coming back from a trip to an important meeting or a big project is bad planning – try and have a calm day to get straight before you take on new work.

It should be pretty clear by now that I believe scheduled work is far more likely to get done than unscheduled work, so why not schedule time to deal with the things that could turn into backlogs if you get distracted? Put an hour in the diary each week to do your filing, or get into the habit of replying to letters and emails when you've scheduled to do it rather than dropping everything as soon as something arrives.

The thing that will really stop new backlogs from mushrooming is developing sensible systems for dealing with incoming work. If you don't have a process for allocating new work, I can guarantee that you are wasting time. New work is often more exciting than existing work just because it's new, and that means we are often more tempted to start work on a new task than complete the one in hand. The result? Inefficiency and time-wasting.

When you are asked, or told, to take on a new piece of work, you need to assess how important it is and the only way you can do that is by asking questions: you need to find out how urgent it is, who it is for, what is expected from you and what help is available. Only then can you assess how long it will take you and find room for it in your schedule.

A good way of dealing with new requests is to let them accrue over the day. When someone asks you to do something, ask them to put it in writing or make a brief note of it yourself and tell them that you will get back to them by the end of the day with a timescale for getting it done. For most people this will be fine, and you then simply look at your collection of requests at the end of the day and schedule them in your diary or add them to your 'to do' list. If something absolutely has to be done that very second, then you should be able to look at your existing work schedule and, because you know how important and urgent each piece of work is, be able to reschedule accordingly. Use your diary to schedule time to deal with each area of your life, and then use your 'to do' list to make sure everything else gets seen to when you have a gap in your schedule.

CHECKLIST

✔ Separate your backlog from new work
✔ Schedule time to deal with your backlog
✔ Start with the newest items on your backlog first
✔ Establish a system for dealing with new work

5
The best way to start your day

I've already told you the story of the entrepreneur who improved the productivity of his workforce by asking them, 'What are you going to *achieve* today?' rather than, 'What are you going to *do* today?'. In the first half of the book, I talked a lot about identifying and securing your long-term goals, but working out your short-term goals is almost as important. How else are you going to achieve what you need to achieve? If you don't plan the day, or week, ahead, it's all too easy to get to the end of the day and feel you've wasted it. Worse than that, you spend the entire day on tasks in the knowledge that you *should* be doing something else.

The solution is brilliantly simple: at the beginning of each day – either when you have breakfast or when you start work – take five minutes to plan your day. Just a few minutes of planning can save countless wasted hours and all you need is your diary – which should have all the tasks in it that you have previously scheduled to do on this day – and the previous day's 'to do' list. All you have to do is schedule as many of the items you added to your 'to do' list yesterday as possible and look to cluster activities where possible, and order your activities logically. I then plan my day by asking a series of questions:

What's important?

Something that wasn't important yesterday can become important today because new information may have caused you to reassess opportunities and threats – remember the SWOT analysis? For instance, you might have been thinking about buying a new computer this year, but an unexpected glitch might make you think you need to start researching new models straight away before your hard drive dies.

When I go to bed tonight, what will keep me awake if I haven't done it?

When I look at yesterday's list to carry over incomplete tasks to my new list, there are always things that I would really rather not do, but I know that if I don't do them they will niggle me and ultimately distract me from the main business of the day. I might not really want to read a report or phone a particular client or respond to a tricky email, but I know that if I don't do that thing, it will (a) have to be done at some point, and that point might end up being less convenient for me, or (b) will have an impact on something else I want to do in the future, or (c) keep me awake at night. Unsurprisingly, these are often the tasks that have been on my list the longest, which is why putting a date on everything that goes on to your list is important. Even if something is relatively minor, if it has been on my list for nearly a fortnight, I make it a priority to get it done.

Why am I doing this?

Sometimes, especially with tasks we'd rather not do, it helps to remind yourself of the end result. Although the process may be tedious or tough, thinking about the eventual pay-off might be more of a motivation. Sometimes we do something that takes us away from our own agenda; rather than being a cause for resentment, it helps to remind you of how other people will benefit from your actions. Maintaining your motivation is key to getting things done efficiently.

How does this help my long-term goals?

Not everything we do fits in with our grand plans, but it helps to remind us every day where we're heading. Asking this question can really help you determine how much time you should spend on certain activities, as something that takes you away from your ultimate goal for too long could jeopardise your dreams. I try and make sure that there is at least one thing on my list each day that moves me towards my goals.

How will I judge my success?

When you are working on a small project, or a tiny task, it is very easy to say when you have done enough, because it is when the project is completed. But for longer projects, how can you tell if you are spending the right amount of time on them? Can you say 'I'll spend two hours on Project X'? Or should you say 'I am going to work on Project X until I have achieved a particular milestone'? The truth is that either could be correct, but the second one is usually more helpful: if we say you're compiling a set of accounts for a board meeting which is in two days' time, then saying you'll work for x hours isn't sufficient. Saying you'll work until you've done half of it is the right way to judge your progress.

■ Employees spend 36 minutes of their working day on personal matters. Men spend longer (44 minutes) than women (29 minutes).
Office Team Survey, 2007

How long will these tasks take?

As I go over my list I jot down an estimate of how long I think each task will take. For activities I've been doing for years, I can be pretty accurate, but for new activities I just have to give it my best guess. I can now see if I can fit everything into my day. If I realise I can't, I look at the tasks that can be done tomorrow.

What's my reward?

If I get everything done on my list, I consider that an achievement worthy of a reward. For me, it's getting to spend more time with my family, but for others it's more time to spend on their first novel, their second life existence or stocking (or drinking!) their wine cellar. Knowing there's a benefit to getting everything done on time is a pretty good incentive for making sure things get done.

Once I've asked myself these questions – and it really only takes a couple of minutes to assess most daily tasks – I am ready to prioritise and plan my day. I can now slot items from my 'to do' list into my diary, making sure that the high-priority tasks are slotted in first. This has two benefits: firstly, I know that I have to get on with the first appointment in my diary otherwise I won't be able to get on with anything that follows – just timetabling the activity has made it far more likely that it will happen; and secondly, when one task is complete, I don't slump into a 'what am I going to do now?' phase where I become unproductive.

Being organised means that, when people ask me to do something, I can tell instantly if I can fit it in. I can see at a glance when I have a window to take something on and I can tell the other person when they can expect me to have it done by. This in turn enables them to plan their day: doing this with all my team means we all work much more efficiently.

There is one last thing I do with my 'to do' list before I get on with my day. I see who needs to know what I'm up to, or who needs to be available for me when I need them to be. There's a chapter coming up shortly about the importance of good communication because letting other people know what you're up to ensures you are not doubling up on tasks or working at cross purposes. So if I can see that my only time in the office will be at midday, I phone ahead and make sure that whoever I need to speak to will be available at midday. Once that is done, I'm ready for anything.

 CHECKLIST

- ✔ Planning your day motivates you to get on with each task: if you fall behind, it's not just the task in hand you jeopardise – it's the whole day
- ✔ Defragmenting your day by grouping together similar tasks speeds things up
- ✔ Sequencing events logically lets you get more done

6
Get organised

Being disorganised is a big waste of time. If you can't lay your hands on documents or information quickly, then small tasks turn into major distractions. Being organised doesn't just free up your time, it also frees up your brain: you no longer have to hold bits and pieces of information in your memory as it is methodically stored elsewhere. Methodical storage also allows you to spot patterns – in your spending, your work rate and your habits – that means you can make timely interventions to stop you from making costly, and time-consuming, mistakes. With so much data at your fingertips, you can make better-informed decisions that will make you more efficient and save you time. When I started my first business, it was in the very early days of computers and I didn't have a clue how to use one, but I bought one anyway because I knew I had to be organised if I wanted to be on top of things. A few hours spent teaching myself to use a spreadsheet saved me so much time in the long run, and that was time I spent growing my business rather than running it.

The great thing about storing information efficiently is that, once you've set up your systems, it hardly takes any time at all to input information and it saves you so much hassle in the long run. And despite what some people might be thinking at this point, setting up your systems in the first place doesn't need to take that long either.

You've probably seen those desk signs that say 'A cluttered

desk is a sign of genius'. Absolute rubbish. A cluttered desk means a cluttered filing cabinet, which means a pile of papers on the floor and an overflowing in tray, which in turn means that that 'genius' is wasting time looking for things that should be easily retrievable. That 'genius' is wasting his single most precious resource. Every so often, in busy periods, paperwork mounts up on my desk, but as soon as I have to spend more than a minute looking for something I know it's time to tidy up. Half an hour spent tidying more than pays for itself in the days that follow.

Once you've got all your information where you can retrieve it easily, you will find something strange happening: you'll feel more confident and assured. Getting organised helps to banish the doubts and insecurities that often slow us down because we no longer worry if we can afford something, agonise if what we're doing is the right thing to do or fret that we have overlooked something important.

What to store

Most of us have crucial documents that would be either time-consuming or costly to replace if we lost them (passport, driving licence) as well as documents that are simply irreplaceable (bond certificates, legal documents, academic certificates). The increasing threat of identity theft makes storing our personal documentation securely even more important.

But it's not just these crucial documents that it makes sense to store in such a way that they can be easily retrieved. Wouldn't it be great if you could easily check your credit card bill against your receipts? Wouldn't it be handy to know how much money you spend each month so that you can decide if you can afford a purchase or not? Wouldn't it make things easier if, at the end of the tax year, you had all your invoices and receipts filed and logged so that filling in your tax return took minutes instead of hours?

If you are self-employed, or run a business, and you invoice clients for the work you do, if you don't keep and file copies of your invoices, how can be sure payment hasn't become over-due? If you issue lots of invoices, it's even possible that you'll forget about the invoice and might never get paid. You are sup-posed to keep your records for six years in case the Inland Revenue wants to investigate you, and just the thought of how awful that would be if you didn't have every receipt should be enough to make you take storing your records seriously.

There are other kinds of information it makes sense to file, too. If you are thinking of buying a new car or a new com-puter you might accumulate a lot of research. You might read online reviews or save special-offer adverts you see in a news-paper. Wouldn't it be great to be able to cross-reference the good reviews with the special offers? If you're organised, this would be a doddle; if you're not organised, you might spend hours looking for the advert in every drawer in your house, and if you haven't stored the online links logically, the chances are you'll never find the same website again.

Alternatively, you might like to keep all your children's school reports so that you can assess their progress; you might like to keep the agreements and terms and conditions your bank or loan company sent you so that you can check that they stick to their side of the bargain. All kinds of documentation is better off stored rather than (a) thrown in a cupboard in no particu-lar order, or (b) thrown in the bin.

■ When you are multi-tasking (answering calls, responding to emails, reading reports), your IQ falls 10 points, the equivalent loss in brain power as losing an entire night's sleep.

Study for the Institute of Psychiatry, 2005

How to store

We now have so many devices for storing information – computers, mobile phones, PDAs, as well as old-fashioned diaries and notebooks – that we can store our information in countless ways. But instead of making things easier, this can actually cause problems. What if you write a date in your diary but don't transfer that appointment to your BlackBerry? More options can create more mistakes: if you file some of your paperwork in a cupboard under the stairs and some of it in a filing cabinet in the garage, how do you know which file is in which place? The secret to effective storage is simplicity.

If you can set aside a shelf, a cupboard or a corner of the loft where you keep all your documents, you will always know where to find everything. All you need after that are a few ring binders, a few boxes and a hole puncher and you can keep all your bank statements, credit card bills and receipts in one place. It will make sense to keep some files in date order and others in alphabetical order. All you have to do is label things clearly.

If you already have a pile of unsorted paperwork, my advice wouldn't be to try and file it all in one sitting: once you have sorted out your system, simply add the old paper to the new system in batches as you find time in your schedule in the same way I suggested you clear your backlogs previously (see pp. 123–7).

It's up to you how organised you want to be. You might want to have one set of records for your personal files but photocopy some of the bills and statements to include them in a household file as well. If you are self-employed, you might need duplicates of some records for tax purposes. If you don't have a photocopier handy you might just want to include a note referring you to the original document in a different file. If you have signed up for paperless billing for your utilities, it's important to print out your bills as, despite technological advances, computers have a habit of crashing and/or becoming obsolete and a paper record will be the only thing that lasts.

There is one big drawback to keeping all your information in actual files on actual shelves as opposed to virtual databases: it is very difficult to back up. Short of photocopying every bill and statement and keeping a duplicate set of records in a storage facility, you are vulnerable to losing vital documents if they happen to get mislaid or you are a victim of a flood or a fire. One solution is to take a high-resolution photograph with a digital camera of every page and store the photo files on your computer, or on a memory stick or external hard drive. It's certainly worth considering doing this for your most precious and vital documents.

Storing information electronically

There are always going to be some files that most of us will want to store electronically, and that means taking a few precautions to guard against the very small risk that you will be a victim of cyber fraud. If your computer was stolen, for example, what would stop the thief from accessing very personal information? Where possible, protect your data using passwords and firewalls. I would also recommend storing your information using some kind of code: a folder labelled 'Accounts' makes it too easy for criminals; labelling your accounts something random like 'Orange' might just keep your data safe. Remember to back up regularly on to a memory stick or CD, but, as these can also be lost, why not see if your broadband provider offers remote storage facilities. That way you can upload your data to their secure database, and if you lost your computer to theft or some kind of malfunction, you would still be able to access your data from your new computer.

When to deal with paperwork

When you deal with your paperwork is as important as how you deal with it. After all, what's the point of having a fabulous filing system if you don't put anything in it? You won't save any time if you still have to scrabble around under your desk for the item that you think is in the third pile from the left.

A pile of unattended paperwork becomes more and more daunting as it grows, and less and less likely to get sorted as we tell ourselves we'll do it some other time. Yet paperwork attended to the moment it arrives on your desk can be almost as time-consuming. A little bit of filing here and there is very inefficient and can distract you from the work you were in the process of doing; you are almost always better off scheduling some time to spend with your files. If you tell yourself that you will spend the first ten minutes at your desk each day on paperwork, or set aside a regular half-hour one evening a week, you can simply put the paperwork that comes your way to one side knowing that it will be dealt with properly shortly. As with other tasks, regular, scheduled sessions will mean you get more done. Not only will your paperwork never spill over into piles under your desk, but you won't be distracted by it in the meantime.

 **CHECKLIST**

✔ Being organised saves you time
✔ Once your systems are set up, maintaining them is quick and simple
✔ Set aside time for paperwork: schedule it, don't do it randomly

7
How to be smart at work

want to spend some time talking specifically about ways we can improve our performance and time management at work. In 2005, the Efficiency in Business Survey discovered some truly worrying statistics: the average office worker loses forty-eight minutes a day to technological failures, e.g. printers jamming and computers crashing; in addition (and this is really quite alarming), they lose an additional two hours a day in pointless meetings, dealing with unnecessary phone calls and staving off annoying colleagues. That's nearly three hours a day, or around 40% of the working day. It seems clear to me that if you can adopt good time-management habits at work, you can transform your productivity, and possibly your career.

Interruptions

Every working day is littered with interruptions and how you handle them can make an enormous difference to how efficient you are. Research for the University of California showed that office workers spend an average of eleven minutes on a task before being distracted. Once distracted, it takes workers twenty-five minutes to return to the original task. Other research shows the average worker is interrupted – by email, phone or colleagues – seven times an hour. What's worse is that 80% of those interruptions are considered trivial.

Learning to anticipate and handle interruptions can transform your productivity, and you can schedule your day so that your interruptions are kept to a minimum. Defragmenting your work into zones when you sort through email, return phone calls, read reports etc means you will get fewer interruptions. If you can schedule your email time in the same way you would schedule a meeting, you will get a lot more done.

■ Office workers are typically interrupted seven times an hour.
80% of interruptions are considered trivial.

Article in Time *magazine, 2004*

Email

The simplest way to reduce the interruptions from email is to close down your email program for most of the day. Instead of being alerted to requests and instructions the moment they are sent (not to mention the YouTube links and Facebook requests), you simply launch your email software at specified times of the day. You can even use the 'Out of Office' reply function to warn your correspondents not to expect instant replies.

As with other tasks, defragmenting the emails you receive into categories – ones that can be easily deleted or ignored, ones that can be replied to in seconds and some that require a bit of thought – can help you deal with them properly. A quick glance will usually be enough to tell you if it's an important email or not and you can file it appropriately. If you can't deal with a request straight away, reply to the sender and say so, then add the task to your 'to do' list.

It's also a good idea to have several email addresses – perhaps one for work, one for friends, one for mailing lists and one for family – and make sure that only the people you should be dealing with at work can contact you at work.

Phone

When you have a deadline and need to concentrate on finishing a task, the phone can be very intrusive. We seem, collectively, to have adopted the mindset that whoever phones us up is more important than the people we're with at the time. So often I see people interrupt important conversations with friends and colleagues to talk to someone on the phone about something that could wait. Whether it's your mobile, your home phone or your work phone, you *don't have to answer it*. In fact, I think there are plenty of situations where you *shouldn't* answer it.

Having Caller ID functionality (where you can see who is calling you) can help you decide if you need to answer. I use Caller ID to capture and store the numbers of a few persistent time-wasters who have got hold of my number. I store them as 'DON'T ANSWER' so that when they call I know not to pick up. Some phones have call-barring features, and you should use them to divert nuisance callers.

Use your answering service message to reflect what you're doing. 'I can't answer the phone right now because I am on deadline. If it is urgent, please call my colleague on . . .', or 'I am currently very busy and can't answer the phone. I aim to reply to all messages within three days, if you need to reach me sooner than that, please email . . .' are both much better than callers assuming you will pick up your messages straight away. As with email, block out a set amount of time in your day to listen and respond to messages.

If you do take a call and it becomes clear that it's going to take you away from your work for too long, you can always ask to call someone back. If you arrange a specific time to call back, you avoid the risk of playing 'answer phone tennis' and endlessly leaving messages for one another. It might even be that by the time you call someone back they have already resolved the issue they were calling you about.

Technology

There are few things more annoying at work than when technology lets you down. Your computer crashes just as you save a precious document; the printer runs out of toner and the stationery cupboard doesn't have a refill; the photocopier insists on copying everything at 50% no matter what button you press: if that sounds familiar, then it is time to get to grips with the technology you use.

Ask your IT department for a tutorial on how to use your computer properly. Most software programs come with tutorials, so why not set aside some time to work through them? You may even find that you discover functionality that helps you save time. When you buy a new gadget, don't throw away the instruction leaflet – work through it methodically instead. If you find that the printer near your desk is always out of ink, tell the person responsible rather than moaning to your co-workers. Or even better, why not become the person who always keeps a spare toner in their bottom drawer and learn how to change it. The less you rely on other people to help you out, the quicker your technology issues will be resolved.

Co-workers

For many people, the best thing about their job is the camaraderie they enjoy when working with a good bunch of people. If you have a tedious job, sometimes the only relief from it is sharing that tedium with someone you can chat to. Sometimes, however, your co-workers can be huge distractions and you need to find ways of minimising their intrusion into your day.

When your boss asks you to do something, you should have such a good idea of how busy your day is likely to be that you know if you can drop everything and carry out the new task immediately. And if you are already up to your eyeballs, you need to say so: 'I have to get x done for our client', or 'The marketing department is waiting for this report and I said I would get it to them today, can we talk about this later?' are fair ways of dealing with ad hoc requests. Just as with unwanted phone calls, make an appointment to get back to your boss to talk about the new project.

When a colleague says to you 'Have you got a minute?' you know they want to take up much more of your time than that. You don't want to seem rude, but you want to be able to get on with your work, so tell them you've got two minutes to spare, see if you like what they've got to say and then decide whether or not to continue the conversation. A good tip is to stand up when someone starts a casual conversation with you: you'll look like you're on your way somewhere and the person talking then tends to talk faster and to be more concise. When you have to work hard, explain this to your co-workers and ask for their cooperation. If possible, work in a meeting room where you won't be disturbed. You can also ask your co-workers to shield you from interruptions so that they can respond to requests, or answer your phone for you; you can do the same for them when they are busy.

■ The cost of not keeping track of your paperwork has been quantified: late fees on credit card payments reached $18.1 billion in 2006. *RK Hammer Advisors, 2007*

Meetings

Most meetings are a huge waste of time. I mean it. Employees often travel great distances and give up valuable working hours just to listen to poorly prepared presentations and to set the date for the next meeting. I might be exaggerating a bit, but we've all walked out of meetings saying 'what was that about?'

Even well-planned meetings can be a waste of time: I sit on the boards of several companies and most of them have far too many board meetings. Why have a meeting to discuss the accounts when we could all be emailed the accounts and study them in more detail in our own time? Often meetings have too many people at them and employees who have nothing to do with, say, the accounts, are given a chance to meddle in the accounts!

In my experience, large meetings can make bad decisions, either because a consensus view is adopted when something more radical would be more effective, or because a dominant personality steers things in his or her direction. I've lost count of the times I've left a meeting for someone to take me to one side to express an opinion they were too shy to share during the meeting. The really bad thing about meetings is that they don't just waste one person's time, they waste several people's time. If you want to get more out of your team, you need to get more out of your meetings.

STEP ONE – Is it really necessary?

First ask yourself if there is a better way of carrying out this piece of business. This is a particularly important question if any one of the parties attending the meeting is travelling a long distance for it. Ask yourself if things would be better discussed over the phone, using Instant Messaging or by email. Would video-conferencing save time and money?

STEP TWO – Setting the agenda

Think hard about what needs to be discussed and what needs to be decided. Work out what you want to get out of the meeting. Think about how long the meeting should take and timetable it. If you start to overrun the timetable, bring the discussion back to the agenda. Chairing a meeting can be nerve-wracking, but if no one else is taking that role on, you should seize the opportunity to ensure the meeting is focused and productive.

STEP THREE – Who needs to be there?

Make sure all the relevant people will be available. There's no point discussing the marketing budget if key members of the marketing team can't make it.

STEP FOUR – Location, location, location

Whenever possible, have meetings as close to you as you can. If you are the person responsible for choosing the location, make sure that you book a suitable meeting space. Will you need AV equipment? Will you need refreshments? Will there be enough chairs? Bad planning guarantees a pointless meeting.

STEP FIVE – Timing

Why do you need to have this meeting now? Is it urgent? Are there opportunities you can exploit by meeting sooner rather than later? Is there a deadline for making a decision? For example, if you are meeting to discuss the budget for a new project, do you need to have it before or after the start of the tax year? Think about the sequence in which events need to happen and make sure that you don't have the meeting too soon, when there won't be enough information available, or too late, when the opportunity has been missed.

You might also want to consider whether the meeting is best held at the beginning, middle or end of the day. Sometimes I find that meetings in the middle of the day can take up more than their scheduled time, especially if you are travelling a long way to get to them. It can be difficult to concentrate on work before you have to leave for a meeting, and there may not be much time left to get on with it when you finally get back to your desk. Early or later meetings are almost always much more time-efficient.

Always state how long meetings are going to last so that those attending can judge if they are going to have time to raise the matters that concern them. If you are worried about meetings overrunning, set an alarm or ask a colleague to come in and tell you they need the meeting room for something else or that your next appointment has arrived.

Over the past few years I have experimented with my meetings after I realised I was spending far too much time in them. My secretary used to schedule my meetings for an hour, but I realised we were spending half that time having tea and exchanging pleasantries, so I started to give people coming to see me a thirty-minute slot, and this worked quite well. The people who came into my office started to be much better prepared as they knew they only had a limited time, but I still felt the meetings weren't as productive as they could be. So I set a time limit of twenty minutes.

It's important that everyone who comes to see me knows they only have a limited time, as otherwise they might spend too long on small talk and not leave enough time for their presentation. At the end of twenty minutes, my secretary phones to tell me I have a call to take, or comes in to let me know the next appointment is waiting: this ensures no one overstays their slot. Since I reduced the time limit to twenty minutes, I have noticed that people are so much more focused and make sure that they make their point very early on in the meeting, giving me more time to question them about their idea or proposal. Famously, Donald Trump has said that no meeting should last more than fifteen minutes. Maybe that's why he's a billionaire; if I can perfect the art of the fifteen-minute meeting, perhaps I'll be a billionaire one day, too!

Food

How many times a day do you stop for a cup of tea, a glass of water or a trip to the vending machine? And when you make these trips, do you find you get distracted or end up chatting to colleagues? While a break from your work could be good for concentration levels, endless trivial snack breaks can really eat into your day. Instead of filling up a glass of water, fill up a bottle and keep that on your desk so you can fill up your glass without going for a wander. Instead of just making tea for yourself, start a 'tea gang' where you all make tea for each other – that way you might only have to make tea once a day. Instead of buying snacks, bring in food from home.

Lunch can often be expensive and unhealthy, not to mention time-consuming, so think ahead about what you will do for lunch. Taking in your own lunch is probably the cheapest, quickest and healthiest option, and that doesn't have to mean soggy sandwiches. If your employer has a microwave and a fridge, you could take in all kinds of meals. Five minutes spent preparing your lunch before you leave for work can save you thirty minutes or more at lunchtime.

Use your lunch break as a motivational tool: tell yourself you will only let yourself go for lunch when you have got certain jobs done. Think about your afternoon's work while you are at lunch so that you return to your desk with a clear idea of what to do next.

■ 59% of middle managers say they miss important information because their company files data so poorly. *Accenture Survey, 2007*

Distractions

Even when we work alone, it can be easy to get distracted by news reports, Facebook, gadgets and games. There are some people who can't stop themselves from having a game (or six) of solitaire and there are others who get a kick out of tinkering with spreadsheets. Recognising and minimising the things that distract you can have a positive effect on your productivity.

What's on your desk?
Are there gadgets and trinkets that you find yourself distracted by? Whether it's an iPhone or a free gift from a client, if you find your hands drifting away from your keyboard towards the distracting object, you know it's time to get rid of it. An uncluttered workspace is usually an efficient one.

What's in your office?
Are there posters, books, CDs, televisions or views that distract you from your work? No one wants to work in a blank cell, but if you know there's something you can't stop yourself from spending time on, then think about decluttering your office.

What's on your computer?
Do you find yourself touching up photos in Photoshop when you shouldn't be? Or sorting out your finances on a spreadsheet when you should be doing your work? Or playing Tetris or solitaire? Computers come bundled up with so much software that there's bound to be a distraction or two on your hard drive. If possible, delete the software that tempts you away from your work, or move it on to a remote storage device so that you have to think twice before opening a program.

How many friends do you have?

I'm talking cyber friends here. Do you spend more time on social networking sites than you do on your work? Are you a news junkie with news 'tickers' scrolling along the bottom of your screen? The internet is the biggest distraction in history and limiting your use of it can transform your efficiency. Ask if your IT department can limit your access. If that's not possible, at least quit your browser software every time you stop surfing. That way you are an extra click away from future surfing and that may just be enough for you to resist surfing the next time you get the urge. As you come across things you would like to look up online, make a note of them and then do all your online work in a single, defragmented session.

 CHECKLIST

✔ **The average worker wastes as much as 40% of their working day on unproductive tasks**

✔ **A planned day is much more efficient than an unplanned day**

✔ **Establish a routine for dealing with incoming work – starting on new tasks straight away can be disruptive**

✔ **Organising meetings properly will make them much more effective**

8
What works for you?

I've already talked about playing to your strengths because when you work with your natural abilities and go with the prevailing current, you can accomplish a lot more, a lot more quickly. I want to expand on that idea now and really scrutinise the situations and circumstances that enable you to maximise your potential for making progress.

To start with, I want you to think about a time when you were really efficient: perhaps a day at the office when you cleared your in tray or took on extra work easily or just did something to a higher standard than usual. Or maybe a day at home when you managed to accomplish more than you had expected to, when you felt on top of things or when it felt as if there had been more hours in the day. If you can't think of such a time, try and imagine a situation where you think you would operate to the best of your ability.

We all get a kick out of being good at something. When we complete a project to a high standard, and especially when we receive recognition for it, it really boosts our confidence, and that confidence enables us to continue doing things well and to get pleasure from doing them. Remembering a time when you felt those things is important because, if you did it once, you know you can do it again – all you have to do is recreate the circumstances that enabled you to excel.

Now I want you to recall a situation when you weren't able to get things done, either at work or at home. Think about the times when you have not been able to settle to a task, or forgot to do something you had promised to do, or ran out of time to do something properly.

What was different in those two situations? You didn't suddenly become a completely different person with inferior skills and a lower IQ, so how can you explain the difference between how you perform in one situation and how you perform in another? If you can work it out, you can replicate the circumstances in which you perform well in other areas of your life so that you always work to the best of your ability.

Over the years I've met lots of people who are super-efficient in the workplace but whose houses are a complete mess. And I know lots and lots of people who will coast along doing the bare minimum until the deadline for a piece of work approaches and then suddenly pull their finger out. It's blindingly obvious to me that, in both cases, people will get away with doing as little as possible until someone finds them out. Seriously: it's only the fact that their boss will notice their untidiness that means they clean up after themselves at work, just as for the others it's only the threat of a deadline – and people realising that they've been slacking – that finally makes them get on with things. If they could find a way of imposing the structure that works for them in one part of their life into areas where they are less successful, they would transform their efficiency and effectiveness.

You need to investigate situations in which you excel and situations in which you fall short of your expectations and see if you can work out why. Once you understand why you achieve more in certain situations, you can then start to recreate an atmosphere that encourages you to perform at your best in every area of your life.

If it's scrutiny that motivates you at work, how can you engineer a greater level of scrutiny at home? If you know that deadlines focus your mind, how can you impose deadlines on other activities? If you know you are easily distracted, how can you remove yourself from the distractions, or remove the distractions from your life?

Sometimes it is the simplest course of action that can make the biggest difference. For instance, if you know you spend too long online, switch to an ISP that offers parental controls and use them (or get someone else in your household to use them) to limit your access to the internet. If you are easily distracted by noise, spending 50p on some earplugs might be all you need to enable you to knuckle down. Just as dieters need to find ways of avoiding cream cakes and biscuits, you need to find ways of avoiding the seemingly insignificant potholes that can make the wheels fall off your day.

■ The biggest time-wasting activities at work are personal internet use (34%), socialising with colleagues (20.3%) and conducting personal business (17%). *Salary.com, 2007*

 CHECKLIST

✔ **Identify situations and circumstances where you perform well**

✔ **Recreate those circumstances in areas where you don't perform as well**

✔ **Removing distractions and imposing deadlines can allow you to perform at your best in all situations**

9
Be decisive

Right at the beginning of this book I said that decision-making is one of the three core skills that enable us to be smarter with our time because indecision is such a big barrier to progress. Hours and opportunities are squandered by individuals and companies just because they are unable to make a decision. I think my ability to make – and stick to – a decision has been central to my success.

I'm tempted to write that I would rather be wrong than indecisive as I think it would get your attention, but it's not quite true. I hate being wrong. However, the fact is that it is because I am *prepared* to be wrong that I am able to make decisions. If you can accept right now that you will be wrong occasionally, and that there's nothing shameful in being wrong every now and then, you will free yourself up to make quicker decisions.

Why are you indecisive?

There is usually a reason why people are indecisive, or go through periods of indecision, and if you can work out the underlying reasons behind your indecision, you can eliminate them. I think indecision has three root causes: (1) habit, (2) lack of empowerment and (3) lack of knowledge.

1 Habit

Making decisions can be a habit, as the more decisions you make, the easier it is to make them. If you get out of the habit of making decisions, or if you've never been very good at making them, you can constantly find yourself being slowed down by indecision. Early on in my career I had so many decisions to make that I did not have time to weigh up all the options and had to rely on my instincts and values to make decisions for me. Before long, I had become a confident decision-maker because I had acquired the decision-making habit. If you don't often get the chance to make decisions, I think this will be a big factor in why you get gripped by indecision when you occasionally have to make a choice.

2 Lack of empowerment

I was out with a friend recently who saw something in a shop window she loved. 'Why don't you buy it?' I asked. Her answer shocked me: 'I don't know if I'm allowed.' She had recently moved in with her partner and they hadn't discussed whether either of them could buy things for the house without the other's consent. I told her this was a classic symptom of a lack of empowerment and that she had to go home straight away and agree the ground rules with her partner. It happens in the workplace, too: if you are standing in for your boss and it falls to you to make a decision that your boss will have to live with, it can be difficult unless your boss has actually empowered you to make a decision. If you've been told something like 'You can authorise any spending under £1000', I suspect you would make those spending decisions more quickly because you have been empowered to do so.

3 Lack of knowledge

Imagine you're going to buy something technical in a field in which you have little or no specialist knowledge, such as a computer, a car or a dishwasher. How are you supposed to know which one to buy? How can you know that the showroom staff are selling you the best product? Having insufficient knowledge is a major cause of indecision and, like the other two root causes listed above, it's entirely understandable why you'd find it hard to make your mind up in a situation like this.

By showing you that indecision is both natural and normal, I hope I can persuade you to stop beating yourself up about dithering and convince you to stop telling yourself that you're bad at making decisions. If you change the underlying conditions, decision-making will start to come naturally. Asking to be empowered to make decisions on behalf of your team, your family or your boss might be all it takes to get the experience of decision-making that you need. Likewise, better research might make your choices much clearer. And the more you practise, the easier you will find it and the better you will be at it.

Now I want to break down decision-making into its component parts. By taking apart the process of decision-making, I run the risk of making it seem more complicated than it is, but I reckon that if you *understand* how decisions are made, you will find it easier to *make* them and quickly realise that these separate steps can all be carried out in the blink of an eye. I believe there are five steps to making good and quick decisions that will help free up time you would otherwise lose:

STEP ONE – Identify the problem

This might sound obvious, but you'd be surprised how often people think they're worrying about A when B is the cause of their grief. In the case of buying a new computer, the problem may be fairly obvious: you need a new computer because the old one is outmoded or broken; but if your problem is a bit more complicated, such as a neighbour who has noisy parties, it might be that the problem is not the noise but the way you react to the noise, or the fact that your neighbour doesn't warn you about the parties in advance. Once you are really sure what the problem is, you are on your way to solving it.

STEP TWO – Identify your objectives

If you can work out what you want from any situation – i.e. identify your goal – then you can plot a route towards that outcome. Let's stick with buying a computer as an example. Ask yourself what's most important: price, design, compatibility, warranty or energy consumption? Once you know what you really want from your new computer, it becomes much easier to select one. With the noisy neighbour situation, ask yourself if you want the neighbour to stop making a noise, only to make a noise at agreed times, to apologise for earlier behaviour or to give advance warning of future parties. Only when you know what you want can you make sure you get it.

STEP THREE – Assess the options

Now you are ready to consider your options. If you were shopping for a computer, you would investigate the specifications and prices of different computers. If you wanted to resolve your dispute with your neighbour, you might take legal advice or talk to the environmental health department at your council or look in online forums to see how others have resolved their disputes.

■ Getting rid of excess clutter would eliminate 40% of housework.
National Soap and Detergent Association, US

STEP FOUR – Assess the consequences

What will be the consequences of your choice? Thinking ahead about how you will feel about your new computer or how your neighbour will respond to your requests allows you to work out if the decision you are about to make will get you what you want. Thinking about how your decision will impact on your life and those around you can help you assess its importance. In business we call this a cost:benefit analysis, where we weigh up the costs of a particular course of action, but also the potential profits if we go ahead. Outside business, it's usually called making a pros and cons list. Simply go through the reasons for and against a particular course of action: seeing them written down can often make your choice much clearer.

STEP FIVE – Make the decision

If you work through the first four steps, the fifth one should come naturally, but I know that's not always the case, especially with important decisions or when you are unused to being decisive. This is why I have some suggestions to help you make your mind up:

- Think of someone you admire and ask yourself what decision they would make. Making the dilemma someone else's can help put it in perspective
- Reduce the time you spend being indecisive by putting a deadline on making your decision
- Reduce the number of options. It's much easier to order from the set menu in a restaurant than the à la carte one. See if you can narrow down the options to just a handful
- Look at your goals. If none of the above has helped you, return to the goals you identified at the beginning of the

book and ask yourself which of the options you are considering takes you closer to where you want to be. When you're
really stuck, let your goals guide you

And if those suggestions don't help you, then I urge you to
remember that being indecisive is almost always worse than
being wrong. And if it does turn out you made the wrong
choice, at least then you will have more information to help
you make better decisions in the future.

 CHECKLIST

✔ Being decisive means being prepared to be wrong
occasionally
✔ Decisions get easier to make the more often you make
them
✔ Isolating the different stages of decision-making can help
you make the right choices
✔ Let your goals guide the choices you make

10
Beware: deadlines approaching

Deadlines are often held up as something of a magic wand for people who have trouble with their time management. 'Stick a deadline on a problem', the theory goes, 'and the problem gets dealt with sooner.' While this is often true, I think there are some circumstances where deadlines can actually create problems because an urgent deadline on an unimportant task can give it a higher priority than a less urgent important task. The result? We become confused about what to give our attention to. There's no doubt that most of us are motivated by a deadline to get things done, but deadlines can actually also make us lazy. Let me show you how. Let's say it's June and your boss asks you to get a project finished for the AGM at the end of September. You calculate that the project will take about a month to finish – what do you do?

(a) Stick it on a Post-it note to remind you to deal with it later?

(b) Start on it right away because you don't have much on at the moment?

(c) Add it to your 'to do' list?

If you chose (a) you run the risk that (i) you will forget, and that (ii) when more work comes your way at the beginning of September you will be rushed off your feet. Someone once told me that deadlines like to hunt in packs: if you don't manage them, a whole lot of them will come at you at once! If you chose (b) you run the risk that external factors will make your project redundant before the AGM. There's also the risk that, because you will be seen as being so efficient, you will be asked to do more work, and that may take you away from your ultimate goals (though if your goal is to impress your boss and gain a promotion, then being keen won't hurt!). If you chose (c) you will spend the next three months thinking about the project; it will niggle away at you and you'll start to resent it, maybe even fear it, but never quite muster the motivation to start on it until the very last possible moment. What's worse is that, because you know you've got a project in the pipeline, you'll take things easy in the meantime. See? Deadlines can make us lazy, which is why we need to learn how to use them properly.

It's often said that we only start work on something when the pain of missing a deadline is greater than the gain of meeting it. Yet without them, businesses wouldn't be able to operate as different members of a team would be working to different timescales and nothing would coincide. So how do we make sure that we use deadlines to motivate us and not demotivate us? Here's how.

Setting deadlines

When you are asked to do a piece of work, how do you know when the deadline for completion should be? Often a deadline is imposed on a project from a higher level, but more often than not you will have a say in when the deadline should be. So how do you successfully decide or negotiate what it should be?

Deadlines work best when they are set for a reason and when everyone involved in a project understands what that reason is. For instance, I am given a deadline to write a book because the publisher needs to schedule in the services of an editor and a proofreader, as well as designers and production staff, ahead of the slot for my book at the printers. If I miss my deadline, I know it will have a knock-on effect for a lot of people and that the publicity campaign planned for the launch will have to be reconsidered, all because I missed my deadline. As an added incentive, I also know that if I keep missing my deadline, the publisher can ask for their money back. Because I understand this, I make sure I meet my deadline.

If my work did not impact on other people's work, how would I set a deadline? Perhaps I would work out how much time it would take me to write this book and make that my deadline. But unless there is a penalty for missing the deadline, or a reward for meeting it, the chances are the book might always stay on the back burner. So when you set a deadline these are the things to consider:

- How long will it take?
- How much time do I have?
- What are the consequences of being late?
- What are the rewards for being on time?
- What else needs to happen before I can start work?
- What else do I need to do during the time this project lasts?

Once you have the answers to those questions, you can work out your deadline. All you have to do then is decide on a contingency – should you add a couple of days, just in case you get ill, or will that just mean that you will fritter away a couple of days, waiting for the threat of missing the deadline to become greater than the gain of meeting it? I sometimes deduct 10% from any deadline because I know it's actually more likely to get done on time. Some people get panicked by deadlines, but if you know how long the work will take and that the deadline is reasonable, I don't see that there's any reason to panic.

■ The three main activities carried out by Britons in 2005 were sleeping, working in their main job and watching TV and videos. In total, these three activities account for 13 hours and 38 minutes of every day. *2005 Time Use Survey*

Shorter deadlines are usually better

I have lost count of the number of times I've been in a meeting and, after a course of action has been agreed upon, the person chairing the meeting has tried to agree a deadline for the work to be done by. Their instinct, more often than not, is to give everyone a deadline so far in the future that no one will be scared by it. 'Excuse me', I find myself saying, 'but I could do this in an afternoon. I reckon everyone round this table could do their bit in an afternoon, too. Why don't we say we can get this done by Friday?' After which there's usually a bit of muttering, most people agree that they can fit the work in and the project happens quickly. A longer deadline for some projects is the kiss of death as it gives individuals involved a chance to pull out or make their excuses or forget about it. I almost always favour a shorter deadline, especially when there are lots of people involved. Even if something isn't urgent, aiming to get things done sooner means the impetus isn't lost and motivation doesn't waver.

Be specific

Deadlines only work when they are specific. Deciding to do something 'by the end of the summer' is almost like saying it will never get done. Deadlines should always have a specific time and date that everyone involved in the project knows about and agrees to. For the project to come in on time, something else needs to be specific, too – the brief. People need to know exactly what is expected of them: the worst thing you can say to someone is 'Come back to me on Friday and we'll see how you got on'. What you should say is 'By our meeting on Friday I need you to have done x, y and z'.

Managing long-term deadlines

Although I've already said that I think shorter deadlines are more effective, some complex projects require longer deadlines. These situations need to be monitored carefully to make sure the objectives – and the deadline – don't drift. If I am overseeing a big project, I meet with the team involved at regular intervals where we can all update each other on our progress and set an intermediate deadline for our next meeting. Intermediate deadlines are crucial to keeping bigger projects on track. It's true for projects that just involve you, too: imagine you have a dissertation to write for your final year at university that needs to be 20,000 words long; you can't possibly write 20,000 words in a day so you need to break it down and give yourself intermediate deadlines of writing a thousand words a day.

When I write a distant deadline in my diary, I also go back a week and write in 'One week to go' and 'One month to go', and when I'm managing a project I email the team involved reminding them of how much time is left. You might also want to consider if you should have a contingency – do you tell your team to get things done two days sooner than is necessary, just in case?

 CHECKLIST

✔ Distant deadlines can make us lazy as we tend to coast towards them

✔ Deadlines need to be specific, and should have penalties and rewards for missing and meeting them

✔ Long-term deadlines need intermediate deadlines so you can monitor progress

11
Overcoming procrastination

've been putting off writing this chapter for weeks. Sorry: I couldn't resist a cheap gag. I've actually been looking forward to writing this chapter because procrastination is, by definition, a complete waste of time, and yet there are some really simple techniques that can get you over a hump and into a period of productivity.

Before I move on to them, I want to discuss the reasons why we procrastinate, because, if we can work out why we're putting off doing something, it's easier to find a solution and get on with the task in hand. Procrastination is almost always a consequence of lack of motivation, which is caused by one of the following:

(a) The task in hand is boring

(b) The task in hand is difficult

(c) We don't see the point of the task in hand

(d) There isn't a big enough reward for getting it done

(e) There isn't a big enough penalty for not getting it done

(f) The task in hand isn't important

(g) We're too busy to pay it enough attention

(h) The task in hand is too big and we don't know where to start

(i) We know we're going to do it badly

In each of these cases, the motivation for dealing with the task is too small to prod us into action or the barriers to getting on with it are too big, so the simplest way to deal with these issues is to find a way of increasing our motivation to get the task done. So the solutions might be:

(a) Doing the task with someone to make it fun

(b) Asking for help

(c) Working out what the consequences of *not* doing it are for you, and for others

(d) Invent a reward – a glass of wine, a double bill of *CSI*, an early finish

(e) Invent a penalty – invite someone to join you for a glass of wine or a double bill of *CSI* and you will probably make sure you meet your deadline

(f) It will be important to someone – work out who and why

(g) By the end of this book, you should find that you have plenty of time

(h) Break the task down into understandable and achievable stages

(i) Accept that you can only do your best and that we can't all be brilliant at everything. Remind yourself of the things you are brilliant at so that you don't get despondent

■ The average Briton spends 87 minutes a day travelling and 82 minutes a day eating and drinking. *2005 Time Use Survey*

It might also help you to weigh up the cost of your procrastination. Sometimes, for instance, if you don't pay a bill on time there is actually a financial cost because you might be hit with interest or late-payment charges, but even when the cost isn't strictly financial it can still be painful: perhaps you will finally be forced into action just as a more exciting opportunity comes along that you will then be forced to forfeit. Procrasti-nation can also impact on our wellbeing as we drag unfinished tasks around us like a ball and chain: knowing that we *should* be doing something is incredibly demoralising. But the biggest cost of procrastination is measured in minutes. Procrastination wouldn't be so bad if we were actually doing something useful with the time we should be spending on the task we're avoiding, but usually we potter and mooch and daydream and fill our time with 'displacement activities' that don't really need to be done. I tell you this for sure: you are not going to lie on your deathbed and say to your nearest and dearest: 'You know what I regret? I really wish I had procrastinated more.' Keep that in mind the next time you're putting something off. Or you could try one of these techniques:

1 Imagine having got the task done and how much better you will feel afterwards. Sometimes this is enough.

2 Write down what's really stopping you from doing it. Sometimes seeing it written down can make it seem so minor and/or absurd that you shame yourself into action.

3 Give yourself a time limit. Instead of saying 'I am finally going to do x today', say 'I am going to spend one hour on x and then I'm going to stop'. As the first hour is often the worst, once you're through this barrier the rest of the task becomes easier. Even saying you are going to spend five minutes on something can get you over the worst. What's even better is that, once you've started doing something, momentum often carries you forward until the task is finished.

4 Just look at the task. Let's say you've had a report in your drawer for three weeks that you can't face reading. Don't tell yourself you're going to read it today, just tell yourself you're going to get it out of the drawer and have a look at it. You never know, you might just find yourself reading a little more of it than you expected to, and then momentum will take care of the rest.

5 Tell someone that you are going to do it and ask them to phone you up or call round later in the day to check that you've done it. If you can buddy-up with colleague or friend to monitor each other, that little bit of scrutiny can force you into action.

The other thing you can do when you find yourself indulging in displacement activities that stop you from doing your real work is to ask yourself one very simple question: does this mindless, pointless activity take me closer to my goals, or further away from them? And then ask yourself a supplementary question: if I keep doing this, will I ever reach my goals? The answers to those two questions should get you back on track!

 CHECKLIST

- ✔ You are not going to look back and say 'I wish I had procrastinated more'
- ✔ Procrastination is usually the result of insufficient motivation
- ✔ There are simple techniques for getting started on a project: momentum often takes care of the rest

12
Communication matters

How are you supposed to do a job well (and quickly) if you haven't been told precisely how to do it? How annoying would it be if your boss said, 'Have you finished that project yet? What do you mean you haven't started? Didn't I tell you I needed it this afternoon?' Would that be more or less annoying than getting home from a trip to the supermarket to find that your fridge was already full because your partner had just done the shopping? Good communication is clearly very important to doing anything and everything efficiently. When we don't communicate clearly workloads are unnecessarily duplicated, colleagues can pull in opposite directions and jobs that don't need to be done take up your time.

There's an old saying: 'What's received is what's communicated'. What that means is that if you can't make yourself understood, it doesn't really matter what you say. To be efficient we need to be able to express ourselves clearly and to ensure that what we've said has been understood. Equally, we have to make sure we properly understand what we are told.

Receiving communication

Imagine you work for an advertising agency and your team is about to visit a potential client for the first time; your boss asks you to do a bit a research into the client. So you have a look at the client's website, you identify what kind of business the client operates, how many employees it has in how many countries and what its bestselling product is. You then show your research to your boss who throws it back at you: 'That's not the kind of research I need: I need to know who their current advertising agency is and why they're switching agencies and how much they've spent on advertising over the past five years.' You'd be pretty annoyed, but who's to blame for you wasting your time on unnecessary research? You or your boss? You both are: your boss should have made it clear what she wanted, and you should have clarified what she wanted before you started work. Receiving communication is as important as issuing it. To make sure you don't find yourself in that situation, you need to have a method for dealing with all incoming communication.

Clarify

Make sure you understand exactly what you are being asked to do. Make sure you understand how your work fits into the bigger picture so that you can liaise with the right people. If there is any part of the brief you do not understand, ask for more information or an introduction to someone who can provide the information.

Specify

Precision saves time, so ask for very specific instructions. If a brickie is asked to build a wall, he needs his client to say more than 'I'd like a wall built, please'. He needs to know where the wall is going to built, how high and what thickness it needs to be, what materials to use and if he will be working alone or if he needs to coordinate his work with the other trades on site.

Deadline

Once you know exactly what is expected of you, you absolutely have to have a deadline for your work. But what if your client demands that a piece of work be done by the end of the day when you have to leave early to pick up the kids and are in meetings until you leave? Then you need to negotiate . . .

Negotiation

If you cannot provide everything you are being asked for in the time frame, you have to say so and explain why. In most situations you should then be able to negotiate the scope of the work, the standard it will be done to or the time it will be delivered by.

Agreement

When both parties agree what is to be done, when, and by whom, then you can confidently get on with the work knowing that the end result will be to everyone's benefit.

■ In Britain, we spent 70% of our time at home.

2005 Time Use Survey

Issuing communication

No matter what kind of organisation you work in, regardless of whether you're the CEO or the tea boy, how you communicate affects how well you work. Good communication skills can compensate for all sorts of other weaknesses: a team that communicates and coordinates its actions is much more effective than a more skilled team that pulls in too many directions at once. Whatever you are trying to say, there are six elements to good, clear communication: who, what, why, where, when and how.

Who?

Who needs to know what you're saying? Think about the person or people you are communicating with: what do you know about them that might impact on what you've got to say? Just as we may simplify our language when we speak to small children so that they will understand us, or modify our language when we speak to important people so that they know we respect them, the tone of your communication should suit the recipients of your message.

What?

What do they need to know? Be as specific as possible. You might also want to think about what they categorically do *not* need to know. Good communication often involves staying tight-lipped when it is prudent to do so.

Why?

Why are you telling someone this? Why do they need to know? Understanding why something needs to be done really can help create the motivation that will make sure it gets done to the right standards and the right deadline.

Where?

There are some messages that are best received in particular places. Intimate confessions, for example, are best reserved for private locations; advertising campaigns for nappies are going to have a better response if they target places where new parents congregate; telling an employee they're fired in front of the rest of the team in an open-plan office is clearly poor practice: whatever your message, consider the context in which it will be delivered. People can be much more receptive to what you have to say if you say it in the right place.

When?

Just as the location is important, so is the timing. If you can see someone is busy, they might hear what you're saying but not have the capacity to take it in and respond to it, and a few minutes later they will have forgotten what you said. The release of commercially sensitive information needs to be particularly well timed: leak it too soon and you may be swamped with enquiries you're not prepared for; announce it too late and you may have lost ground to a rival.

The other aspect of timing is agreeing a deadline, especially when you are trying to get a group of people to coordinate. When you ask for a piece of work to be done but don't attach a deadline to that work, the chances are that it will not get done.

How?

If you ask someone nicely, do you think they are more likely to do what you want than if you bark at them? Actually, that depends: some people need to be shouted at to get them to take situations seriously (you're not going to say, 'Oh, by the way, I thought you would like to know that your house is on fire', you are going to say 'Fire! Get out!'), whereas some people need to hear encouraging tones. Thinking about how you will deliver your message makes a big difference to the response you'll get.

When you are asking for work to be done, you also need to consider how you want it to be done. If you are a confident delegator you may not care, so long as it is done to the specified standard by the specified date, but even then you might still care about the methods used. For example: if you are using builders, do you care if the materials they use are ecologically sourced, or that they don't start work before 9.00 a.m. so as not to disturb your children? There is usually more than one route to every destination, and if you want someone to take a particular road, then you need to spell it out.

 CHECKLIST

- ✔ A team that communicates and coordinates its actions is much more effective than a more skilled team that pulls in too many directions at once
- ✔ What's received is what's communicated: make sure you have been understood
- ✔ When communicating follow the rules of who, what, why, when, where and how and your message will be understood

13
Be a smarter commuter

The average commute to work in the United Kingdom is thirty-five minutes each way. Ten per cent of British commuters spend more than two hours a day travelling to and from work. For full-time workers, that's about three and a half days a month! Unless you are commuting to a job that fulfils you, every minute of that journey is spent moving away from your goals.

It's not just time-consuming: commuting can be expensive, stressful and exhausting, not to mention unpleasant when you are shoved nose to armpit on some of the busiest commuter routes. Clearly, the less time you spend commuting the better.

Reducing your commute

If you have a long commute (and, for me, that's more than an hour each way) have you ever stopped to ask yourself something pretty fundamental: why? Seriously. Why did you accept a job that was so far from where you live? Or why did you choose to live somewhere so far from where you work? A long commute is easier to endure if you know why you're putting yourself through it. The high cost of property – despite the recent financial turmoil – means that many people work in cities and commute in from beyond the suburbs where property is cheaper. If that's something you're happy with then fine, but did you consider living somewhere smaller that's nearer to where you work? You'll never get your time back, and you can always move out to the country when you retire.

I recently bought a flat in London and I was determined it should be as central as possible so that I could use the flat as an office. I have most of my meetings there and the ones I have to leave the flat for are usually within walking distance. I could have bought a much bigger place in the suburbs, but location was far more important to me. It's an idea I got from reading one of Donald Trump's books: when he built Trump Tower in New York he made sure his apartment was right above his office so that he wouldn't have to commute!

If you're not about to move house or change jobs, the next question to ask yourself if you have a long commute is: when did you last change the way you commute? Have you experimented with taking different routes or trying later or earlier trains? There are three routes I could take to get from my house to my HQ in Darlington and I've timed each of them. One takes twenty-four minutes, one takes twenty-three minutes, – I take the twenty-minute route.

Over the years I've heard a few stories of commuters taking the same train and not even realising that an express service had started, or the same roads not realising a by-pass had been built! In London, a friend of mine only discovered the river-boat service when there was a Tube strike: he'd never got to work so quickly and now he takes it every day. There hadn't been a riverboat service when he'd started his job and he'd never thought to investigate alternatives until he was forced to. Check out sites like the AA's route planner (www.theaa.com) and Transport For London (www.tfl.gov.uk) for suggestions on your quickest commute. Most regional transport authorities have similar route-planning services.

■ On average, men spend 13 minutes a day cleaning and tidying, compared to women, who spend 47 minutes on those tasks. Men spend 23 minutes a day on 'repairs and gardening', while women spend 11 minutes on these activities. *2005 Time Use Survey*

There were a couple of guys who used one of my health clubs who always started their workouts at 7.30 a.m. I knew from membership records that neither of them lived nearby, so I asked them why they were always at my club so early. They both said that if they left home at 7.00 a.m. their commute took half an hour. If they left at 7.30, it took them an hour because the traffic was so much worse. By leaving earlier, they found the time for a workout they might not otherwise have managed. Changing the time of your commute can make it quicker (and if it's out of peak time, it'll also be cheaper on most public transport).

The next way to reduce the time you spend commuting is to reduce the number of times you do it. Do you work for a company that supports flexible working? Could you, for instance, work four long days rather than five regular days? If you commute by car, this will also save on petrol, which in turn helps reduce your carbon footprint. Or could you negotiate to work one day a week from home? Over the course of a year, this will enable you to reclaim lost commuting time for something more useful.

Making your commute count

If you can't reduce the amount of time you commute, you might be able to combine your commute with another activity and so get more from each day. Here's my list of things you could do while you commute:

Exercise

Could you run, walk or cycle to work? Perhaps not every day, and perhaps not both ways, but if you can incorporate exercise into your commute you will save money, burn calories, reduce your carbon footprint and feel great.

Work

A journalist called Douglas Jackson used his hour-long train journey into his job on the *Scotsman* newspaper in Edinburgh to write a novel. He got a two-book deal for his efforts. What could you do while you're sitting on a train or a bus? I always catch up on my reading when I take the train, and thanks to my BlackBerry I can respond to emails or write my column for the *Daily Telegraph*. If you can prove to your boss that you use your commute to work advantageously, this might help with future negotiations over working hours or salary. If you know you always get a seat on the train and you have a laptop, you might be surprised how much you can achieve.

Recreation

Mobile broadband and WiFi now make it possible to use the internet almost anywhere. So if you catch the train or bus to work, instead of using your work time to surf, you could do it on the move. Services like the BBC's iPlayer means you can catch up on TV you missed, and if your laptop plays DVDs, you could even spend your commute watching TV or a film rather than doing that when you get home. Even if you never get a seat or are at the wheel, there are now so many download-able podcasts of radio shows and audio books that you could at least be listening to something useful.

Relaxation

I know some people who really value their commute. They tend to be parents and they tell me that their commute is the only time they get to themselves. Being between places means they can relax. Whether they read for pleasure, meditate or even sleep, it's something that wouldn't get done otherwise.

 CHECKLIST

✔ Can you reduce your commute by changing your route or your mode of transport?

✔ Can you commute less frequently?

✔ Technology means you can combine your commute with work, or use the time to do something fun

14
Teamwork

Teams can achieve more than individuals in a shorter space of time. Whether you manage a team or are part of a team, getting your team to work together can transform your achievements at work. In good teams, people with complementary skills work together, each playing to their strengths, and each recognising the strengths of the other team members. In good teams, tasks are carried out simultaneously rather than consecutively, and aims and objectives are reached much more quickly. Without teamwork, certain tasks are inevitably duplicated, knowledge is not shared and people waste time on tasks they are not good at. Many of the benefits of teamwork are the same as the benefits of delegation, and it may help to turn back to page 51 and look again at the chapter on Delegation. Here are my five tips for better teamwork:

TIP 1 – Play to your strengths

Work out what you are best at and find a role that allows you to excel. Is there one area of your firm's work that excites you more than others? Can you become an expert in a particular field? Ideally, each member of the team should have different areas of expertise; so what's yours going to be? Even within specialist teams, wouldn't it be great if someone took responsibility for the stationery while another person took responsibility for updating the intranet? Find your niche within your team and you will acquire competence and experience that will mean things get done more quickly.

TIP 2 – Recognise other team members' strengths

There is always a risk that the technology expert in a team thinks the only important element of the team's work is the technology. Just as the marketing guy thinks marketing is the most important element, so of course the guy in accounts thinks marketing is easy. The truth is, it's only what the team achieves that counts, so everyone's contribution is equally vital. The creative genius who only seems to do a few minutes' work each day should be valued for his contribution, just as the diligent administrator who takes care of filing and paperwork should get your respect.

TIP 3 – Help each other

In most companies and in most teams there will inevitably be times when one person is busier than his or her colleagues. Wouldn't it be great when you were rushed off your feet if one of your colleagues helped you out? If you ask yourself two questions – what can I do for my colleagues? and what can they do for me? – on a regular basis, you will help each other perform better.

TIP 4 – Coordinate

Good teams are well balanced. If you have five leaders in your team, the chances are that not much will get done. Ditto if you don't have a leader at all. Good teams have a mix of talents – you need a leader, a creative person who can come up with solutions, you need a salesperson who can shout about the team's achievements, you need people who can take a brief and be trusted to get on with their work, you need interpreters who can see the practical applications of the creative people's innovations, you need people who pay attention to detail and you need people with enquiring minds who will investigate and analyse ideas. And these skills come on top of your professional skills and sector expertise. There's no point in a group of technological whizz-kids coming up with a clever new computer program if there's no one on their team who can see the practical applications or who has the vision to sell it to a customer.

TIP 5 – Communicate

It's all very well you deciding that you're going to be the leader of your team, but what if your colleagues don't agree? You might think you're doing vital research that will help everyone, but what if your colleagues think it's a waste of time? The best teams share information – what they know, what they're doing, what their customers are doing – to ensure that each member is working towards the same goal. Regular meetings, email updates and open-plan offices can all help improve communication. If there's someone on your team whose work you don't properly understand, go to lunch with them and find out what they do. You might discover that you've been duplicating tasks, or pulling in opposite directions, or that you could really help each other out.

■ The average worker spends almost an hour a day looking for documents that have been inefficiently filed.

2009 research for Canon

CHECKLIST

✔ Teams can achieve more than individuals in the same space of time, but . . .

✔ . . . uncoordinated teams can pull in several directions at once

✔ Good communication means everyone pulls in the same direction

15
Technology

Laptops, BlackBerrys and mobile phones mean it is now possible to work pretty much anywhere. The time we used to spend between places can now be used productively. Some people might think that's a bad thing, but if you want to save time these gadgets are a big help.

I am able to oversee the running of my companies from my villa in the South of France because my team know they can get hold of me whenever they need to. My BlackBerry means I can read and approve crucial documents from the poolside or reply to emails while I'm on the train.

Technology can do a lot of administration work for us: names and numbers are automatically stored alphabetically, contacts on hand-held devices can be automatically synchronised with a database on your computer, and, unlike a diary, they can sound an alarm to tell you your next meeting is in ten minutes' time. And unlike standard diaries, which tend just to be for a calendar year, you can slot in dates much further into the future. Whether it's when you need to reapply for a passport or book flights for next year's annual conference, iCal, Palm and Entourage software is a lot more flexible than a paper diary.

Whatever devices you rely on, learning to use them properly is essential. There's no point wasting time every time you send a text trying to work out how to check the spelling! And there's no point having a phone book of several hundred names of people you can't remember. When I store a new name in my phone, I always list it with the organisation they work for. For instance, the production team on *Dragons' Den* are listed as 'DD Dominic', 'DD Karen' etc because I know if it just said Dominic or Karen I wouldn't instantly know who was calling and might not take the call. Likewise, I know several men called Peter so they are listed in my phone book as 'TwoFour Peter' or 'Moujins Peter' as that's how I think of them. When I want to contact TwoFour productions, who make some of my TV shows, I can see the names of the team in a single list. And if I want to invite my neighbours at my villa in Moujins round for drinks, I can see all their numbers at a glance. Learning to program your devices to suit your needs means that you will be in control of the technology and not the other way round!

It's understandable why some people think that the solution to their time shortage is technological, but, in their quest for the perfect gadget that orders a new pint of milk when a microchip in their fridge tells it they're running out, they forget that technology is only as smart as the person who uses it.

■ 16% of UK workers fail to take their full holiday entitlement each year. The typical number of days not taken is 3. On a salary of £24k, that's like giving your boss a £300 bonus!

2009 Survey for Teletext Holidays

The pitfalls – and how to avoid them

1 Too many devices

If you have a mobile phone, an iPod Touch and a computer, where are you going to store all your important information? Are you going to miss appointments because you entered them in the wrong device? Are you going to flounder in a meeting because you left the device with your presentation on it at home? If you are going to juggle different devices, you need to establish a really clear system for inputting data on to them. It makes sense to buy compatible devices, but, even then, they won't automatically sync information unless you remember to hook them up so that they can talk to one another.

2 It's too easy to lose data

Whether it's because you left your BlackBerry on the train, or you spilled coffee on it, or a virus wiped its memory, there will come a time when the benefits of having a paper copy of everything will be obvious. You need to be diligent about making back-up copies of important files.

3 Obsolescence is inevitable

Gadgets only stay shiny and new for a very short period of time. Sometimes it seems that as soon as you've bought a piece of technology it's out of date. Apart from the cost and the waste, this creates another problem – at some point the device you rely on is going to become incompatible with another device you rely on, or its battery is going to stop charging properly, which means you can't take it anywhere with you. The only solution is regular upgrades: some mobile phone companies offer 'free' upgrades as part of your service subscription.

4 You need an IT department on permanent standby

If you are not very technically minded, what will you do if your device starts playing up? Whenever you buy a new gadget, make sure you know what kind of technical support you get with it and ask for a tutorial on how to use it. Make sure you spend some time reading through the instruction leaflet and that you know how to fix minor problems yourself.

5 You can never switch off

If you can get on with work anywhere, anytime, then there's a pretty good chance that you will end up working a lot longer than nine to five. The lines between your home life and your work life become blurred, and you remain on alert for longer knowing that colleagues could get in touch at any moment, or that you could just get on with that report. If that sounds like you, perhaps getting a second phone/BlackBerry for work is a good idea. That way you can switch it off when you get home knowing friends and family can still contact you on your other number. My team know only to call me after 9.00 p.m. if it's an absolute emergency: anything else can wait until the morning. Perhaps you need to agree similar boundaries with your colleagues.

For me, the downsides of always being 'on call' are easily outweighed by the benefits: if I can read reports and respond to emails while I'm on holiday, it means I can take longer holidays!

 **CHECKLIST**

- ✔ Technology and gadgets now mean we can work anywhere
- ✔ Gadgets only save us time if we know how to use them properly and can resolve hitches ourselves
- ✔ Establish a routine for making sure data on gadgets is backed up

Duncan's personal Top Ten time-wasters!

1

Watching rubbish telly
Seriously, you are not going to look back on the time you spent on your sofa and think it was well spent!

2

Watching 24-hour news
I can't get over how many people put twenty-four-hour news channels on waiting for the headlines or the story they are following. Press the red button and read the headlines on the text service. And then get on with your day.

3

Looking for documents that haven't been filed properly
It is so frustrating when you are on the phone with someone who says, 'Hang on a minute, it's just here, no, it's in this pile, I won't be long . . .' Just get a system together and USE IT!

4

People who get to the front of the queue at airport security
. . . and THEN start emptying their pockets, taking watches off, getting laptops out etc – why can't they do this while they're in the queue?

5

EasyJet passengers who board first and sit at the front
If you started boarding from the back, we'd all get on sooner and we'd take off on time!

6

Entrepreneurs and inventors . . .
. . . who start their pitch saying: 'My idea is the biggest money-making idea you'll ever hear . . .' It never, ever is.

7

Roadworks, roadworks
. . . and more roadworks.

8

Glitches on my computer and so-called 'go faster' broadband
Why can't they make computers that don't crash? Why are broadband services still so unreliable?

9

Slow cars in the fast lane
Not only are they annoying, they are dangerous. Just pull over and let the rest of us overtake you without having to bunch up behind you.

10

Waiting for my wife to get ready
(although the end result is always worth it!).

So, what are you doing today?

Index